THE ART AND CRAFT OF
TEA

Joseph Wesley Uhl

THE ART AND CRAFT OF TEA

an enthusiast's guide to selecting, brewing, and serving exquisite tea

Quarto is the authority on a wide range of topics.

Quarto educates, entertains and enriches the lives of our readers—enthusiasts and lovers of hands-on living.

www.QuartoKnows.com

First published in the United States of America in 2016 by
Quarry Books, an imprint of
Quarto Publishing Group USA Inc.
100 Cummings Center
Suite 406-L
Beverly, Massachusetts 01915-6101
Telephone: (978) 282-9590
Fax: (978) 283-2742

Visit our blogs at
www.QuartoKnows.com

10 9 8 7 6 5 4 3

ISBN: 978-1-63159-049-8

Digital edition published in 2016
eISBN: 978-1-62788-315-3

Library of Congress Cataloging-in-Publication Data
Uhl, Joseph, author.
The art and craft of tea : an enthusiast's guide to selecting, brewing, and serving exquisite tea / Joseph Uhl.
pages cm
ISBN 978-1-63159-049-8 (hardback)
1. Tea. I. Title.
TX817.T3U39 2015
641.3'372--dc23

2015025839

Design: Burge Agency
Photography: Marvin Shaouni

Printed in China

To Erwin R. Uhl, for directing me to plant seeds and saplings wherever I damn well please.

CONTENTS

PREFACE

As one of the most consumed beverages in the world, tea is virtually everywhere. But, what exactly is tea? Is it a drink? A diet drug? A cure for cancer? A gateway into mysticism? A skin balm? Is it a flower? An herb? Or, is tea just another consumer-packaged product?

I wrote this book to start a dialogue about how to define tea, to help clarify fact from myth, and to outline the importance of tea not only in world history but in our own lives. My hope in writing this book is that it sheds light on much of tea's complexities.

If you are a serious tea drinker, a casual tea drinker, or someone merely curious about one of the world's great crafted agricultural products, this book should provide something of value and interest. Throughout the book, I tried to remain aware that tea's power and magic is not found in its leaves, in the liquid it creates, or in our relationship to these things, but in its ability to help us feel connected to our shared humanity.

PART 1: TEA

WHAT IS TEA?

Tea started in the northern foothills of the Himalayan mountains where people chewed the leaves of the Camellia sinensis plant as medicine. Over the past few millennia, the Chinese invented techniques and technologies that allowed them to preserve these leaves. In so preserving the leaves, the Chinese created technologies that not only allowed the leaves to last longer but allowed tea to be transported greater distances. With the increased transportability of tea, new villages began cultivating tea and began creating their own proprietary techniques and technologies for the processing of tea. This long history of creating, sharing, and innovating created the various types of teas with which we are now familiar as well as the hundreds if not thousands of varieties of tea that can be enjoyed today—all from a single leaf!

THE HISTORY OF TEA AS A CULTURAL ICON

It seems an unwritten rule that a book about tea shall begin with a series of dates and events representing tea's history.

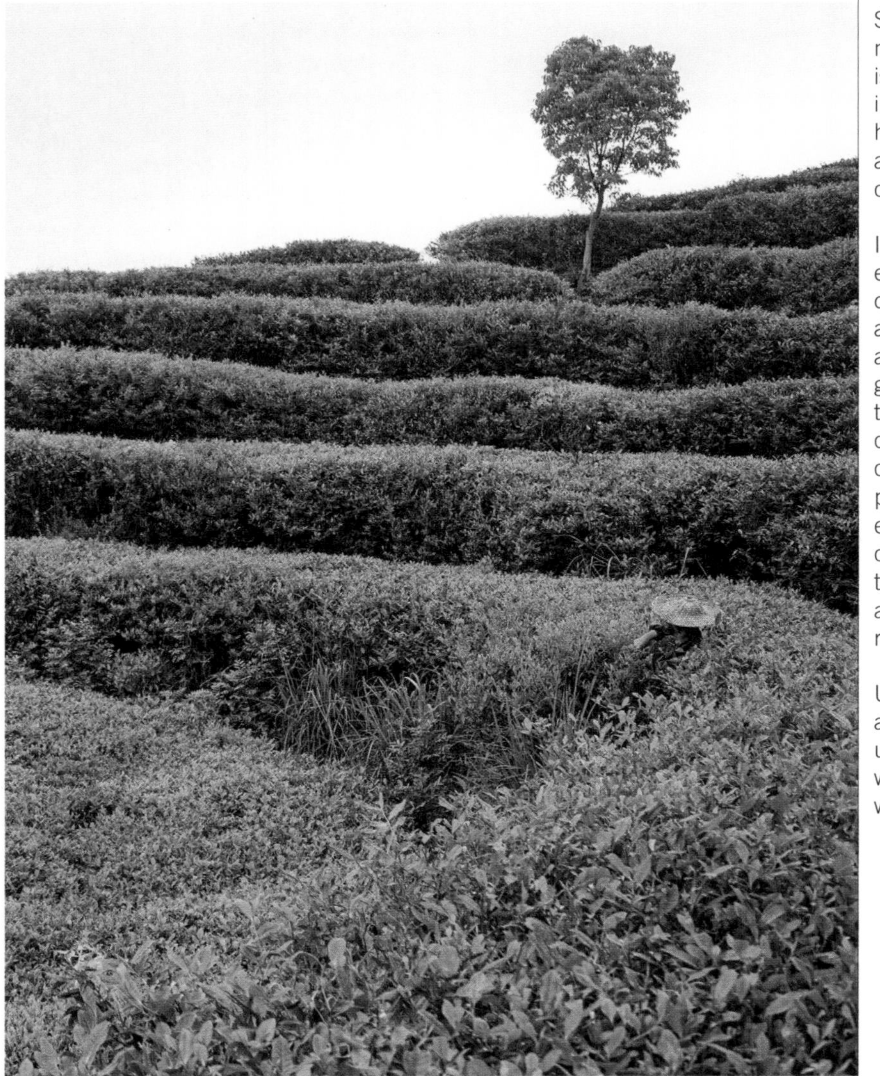

Such an exercise, however, misses the mark in helping us understand what tea is. Tea's history cannot be distilled simply into a series of dates and events. Its history is as complex, rich, and colorful as the number of tea servings consumed over the past three thousand years.

In fact, tea's complex history changes every time someone: drinks a new tea; drinks tea for the first time; drinks a tea and experiences an epiphany or feels a deeper understanding about himself; gifts a canister of tea to a friend; feels the world slow down after drinking a cup of tea; thinks "I wish I drank more tea"; or states "I don't drink tea—I'm not a tea person," etc. Only because of these felt experiences are we motivated to drink or decline a cup of tea, to invite a friend to share a cup of tea, to travel the world and learn how people prepare tea, or to read books about tea.

Understanding these felt experiences and our beliefs about tea helps us understand tea's "history"—for in a real way those experiences and beliefs are what make tea tea.

STORIES AND MYTH-OLOGY

Although the history of tea is as great as the summation of all of the tea consumed, the story of tea, as it is most often told, invariably begins with one of a handful of genesis myths. These myths are good stories but, more important, they provide significant insight into the cultural importance of tea throughout the world.

CONFUCIAN ORIGINS

One of the more popular of these myths, and the first story I heard told about tea, starts with the Chinese inventor of farming and medicine, Shennong, sitting in the shade of a Camellia Sinensis tree. While Shennong sat under the tree, a leaf allegedly fell into his cup of boiled water and began to steep. Being a man of medicine, Shennong noted that the leaf not only created a beautiful green color, but that it made him feel refreshed, stimulated, and full of vigor. Thus, tea was born.

This Chinese myth is important not because it describes the origins of tea, but because it helps link the present to the mythical past and reminds us of the power and security of ancestry. This fable guides us into seeing the world through a Confucian lens and provides a glimpse into the Chinese worldview and their reverence toward tea.

BUDDHIST ORIGINS

Another genesis myth that has repeatedly been shared with me provides that the founder of Buddhism, Siddhartha Gautama, sat down after a long meditative walk through the mountains and unwillingly fell asleep. When he awoke he felt furious at his lack of control and discipline, and at his weakness. So, in a fit of rage he ripped out his eyelashes and threw them into the wind. From these eyelashes grew the first tea plants.

Like the aforementioned Confucian fable, this myth provides a glimpse into a particular worldview. Generally, the myth illustrates the fundamental Buddhist belief that one cannot find true enlightenment until one has escaped the bonds of the material world—an idea represented by the Buddha's removing of his eyelashes. Interestingly, it has been stated that tea's ability to provide energy and focus made it the perfect accompaniment to the intellectually rigorous demands of Buddhism and is what helped Buddhism spread from south Asia through all of Asia. Similar to the Confucian myth, this myth is not just a story about the origins of tea; it is a lesson that guides us into understanding the Buddhist worldview and their reverence toward tea.

WESTERN EUROPEAN ORIGINS: A STORY IN THREE ACTS

If you read a book about the history of tea from an English or Dutch perspective, the stories are usually tied to the creation and expansion of empire: espionage, development of a modern navy, treasure hunting, drug trading, and the accumulation of wealth. These stories are critical to confirming the worldview of Europeans, where they fit within that world, and how they relate to tea. They also help demonstrate tea's cultural status to Western Europeans as well as provide insight as to how the Western world conceptualizes tea.

ACT 1—THE INTRODUCTION OF TEA

Most books about the history of tea in Europe begin sometime around 1600 when England created the East India Company, an organization with authority to acquire territory, coin money, maintain armies and forts, form foreign alliances, and declare war. Through these powers the East India Company started trading silver for tea in the late 1600s and began to acquire large wealth for the English Crown.

The East India Company was so successful trading tea, however, that by the middle of the 1800s England's silver reserves were virtually depleted. To fix this imbalance, the East India Company tapped into its resources from land it acquired in Bengal—namely large fields of poppy plants, the seeds of which could be used for processing opium—and began trading opium for tea, a practice that resulted in severe opium addiction throughout China in the 1800s, the two famous Opium Wars (1839–1842 and 1856–1860), and, eventually, the cessation of Chinese foreign trade. With trade between China and the West virtually stopped throughout most of the 1900s, the tea industry was forced to become creative in order to sell "tea." Thus, it became more common for tea companies to market products such as flowers, herbs, spices, and so on, as "tea."

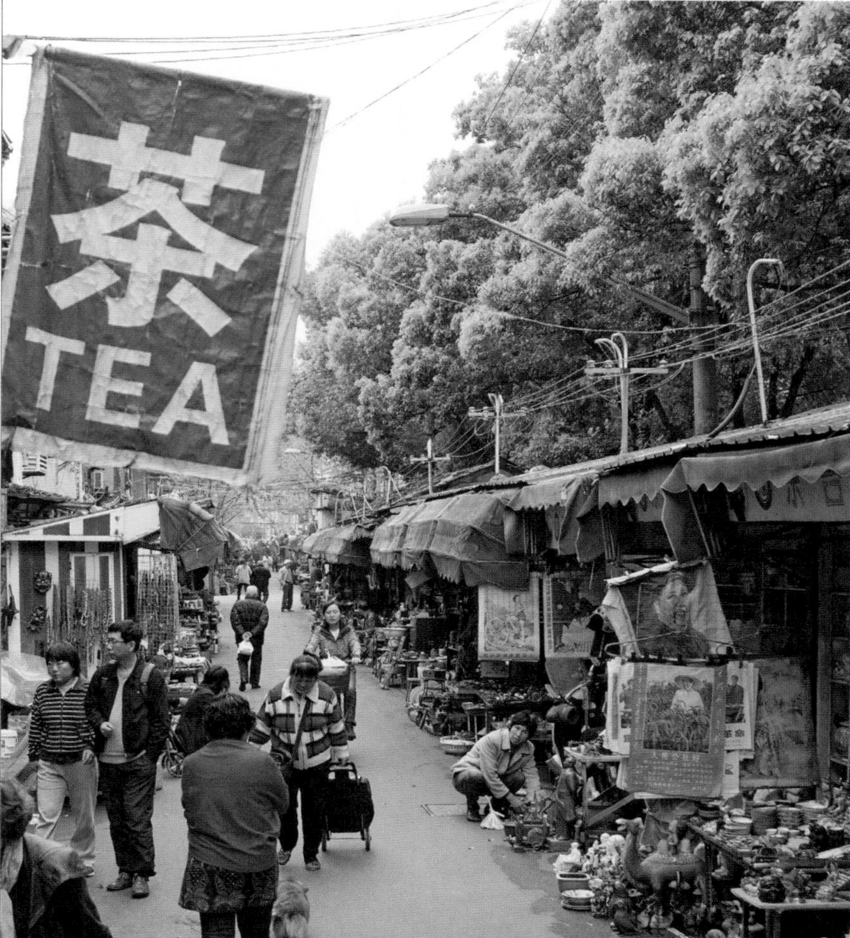

The irony that the English sought to acquire tea by enabling opium addiction throughout China seems to be lost in most discussions about tea in the Western world, but it is fundamental in understanding current tea trends.

It is generally agreed that the Opium Wars were the precursor to the demise of Imperial China; that the vacuum left from this political instability eventually led to the Chinese Communist Revolution; that the Communist Revolution led to China's Cultural Revolution in the 1960s; and that these revolutions almost completely destroyed China's specialty "bourgeois" tea industry.

With trade between China and the West stopped, generations of people in the Western world could no longer experience China's famous teas. Only after the Chinese began liberalizing its trade restrictions in the 1980s and 1990s did the Chinese tea industry begin to recover and did the Western world again begin to discover the joys of these teas. Thus, in the past fifteen to twenty years the world is again beginning to "discover" the great Chinese teas.

ACT 2—THE CREATION OF A COMMODITY

Prior to using opium to extract tea from China, the British governor general of India began investigating whether it was possible to break China's tea monopoly by growing tea in India. In anticipation of this experiment, he annexed what is present-day Assam (1824) and purchased a deed from the raja of Sikkim for land around the present-day region of Darjeeling in the state of West Bengal (1835).

In 1834, the English began propagating tea in their new territory of Assam. They propagated this area not with the *Camellia sinensis* var. *sinensis* plant (as is most often used in China) but with a plant growing indigenously in Assam, a different variety of *C. sinensis* called *C. sinensis* var. *assamica*. (Although *C. sinensis* var. *assamica* is just another variety of tea, it has important physiological and chemical differences from those of the variety *C. sinensis* var. *sinensis*, differences that create a more bitter and astringent tea.)

England's new south Asian tea experiment was met with much nationalistic fervor, and the English dreamed of a day they could control the entire tea market and no longer be subjected to the Chinese control of production. In 1839, a mere five years after propagating tea in Assam, the first Assam black tea was auctioned in London.

Although the London tea tasters evaluated these leaves as merely "of reasonable quality," the novelty and nationalistic enthusiasm of the moment was extraordinary and the English's marketing machine helped spur record tea prices. In fact, the English felt so much enthusiasm for growing tea in India that, according to *For All the Tea in China: How England Stole the World's Favorite Drink and Changed History* by Sarah Rose, the last lot of tea sold at that auction (the lot reserved for the lowest quality leaves) fetched a higher price than the earlier lots, selling for approximately $168 per pound (an extremely high price for most teas sold in England today). Alas, the base for all current English black tea, including the ubiquitous black tea blends English Breakfast and Earl Grey, was born, and Western tea companies found a new means of creating higher profit margins. They now owned the production of teas that they successfully marketed and sold at "premium" prices.

I write these anecdotes not to describe meticulously all the events that influenced the development of tea in the Western world but to develop the theme that, unlike many Asians who often conceptualize tea as a way of life, most in the West have historically viewed tea as a commodity. Tea trade in Western countries has rarely been about acquiring a well-crafted drink, an elixir of life, or a means to self-fulfillment; tea has generally been just another product marketed to acquire wealth. Grasping this difference is fundamental in understanding how people around the world view and conceptualize tea differently and helps explain why the world has a difficult time explaining what "tea" is.

ACT 3—THE EMERGENCE OF BLACK TEA IN THE WEST

At precisely the same time that the English were beginning to create the south Asian tea industry, the English discovered that the Chinese tea processers were using Prussian blue and yellow gypsum to make their tea leaves appear more green, appeasing the world's preference for perfectly green leaves. Prussian blue is a deep blue pigment used in painting and dyeing, but it is also a pigment that contains arsenic! Needless to say, the discovery that they were slowly being poisoned while drinking green tea had a long-lasting chilling effect on Europeans' green tea consumption.

Furthermore, although the West had traded tea with the Chinese for almost three hundred years, by the time they discovered most of their green tea contained arsenic and by the time the English created their fledgling tea industry in south Asia, the English had yet to discover that black and green tea were made from the same plant! It was not until 1843 that the English made this realization—four years after the first Assam tea bubble. It is no wonder that the Europeans and the people of their old colonial states drink black tea today! Had the English simply realized that they could have used the leaves growing in India to create green teas, our assumptions about tea and tea culture in the West might look much different today.

A BASIC UNDER-STANDING OF TEA

The story of tea in the West over the last 150 years is important not only to illustrate our relationship with tea, but also to explain current market conditions. For instance, if you walk through the aisles of a contemporary grocery store or peek into a typical modern kitchen, you might be deluded into believing that tea is a dried herb, a blend of spices, or a collection of dried flowers or fruit.

Unlike these often-mislabeled tisanes and aromatics, tea is something altogether different. It has a unique history, comes from designated growing regions, and uses manufacturing processes not used in the creation of any other agricultural products. These unique attributes enabled the creation of thousands of types of teas all made from an extraordinary evergreen plant from the sinensis species in the genus Camellia of the Theaceae family in the plant kingdom: Camellia sinensis, or simply tea!

Although all tea comes from the Camellia sinensis plant, all tea is not created equally. Tea is typically divided into six subdivisions or types: white, green, yellow, oolong/blue, black/red, and dark/fermented (I refer to black/red tea as black tea and dark/fermented tea as dark tea). Each type of tea, in turn, is defined by the specific processing used to create it. To make any given tea, there are essentially eight steps that must take place: plucking, sorting, cleaning, withering, manufacturing, firing/drying, sorting, and packing. Whether a tea is classified as a white tea, a green tea, or a dark tea will rest solely on how the tea was manufactured.

PROCESSING

Without question, the most influential variables for how a tea tastes, smells, and appears are the processes used to create the tea.

Oxidized teas such as black tea and partially oxidized teas such as oolong tea are drastically different in their taste, aroma, and appearance than unoxidized teas precisely because of the oxidation process the leaves of those teas undergo. Similarly, and as explained in "Steaming" in the Types of Tea chapter (page 31), if a tea master decides to steam a green tea instead of pan frying or baking it, he will dramatically change how the tea tastes, smells, and looks. Steaming creates a bright and vibrant green appearance and an unmistakable grassy flavor, whereas pan frying creates a tea with a dull green hue and a roasted and nutty flavor. These processing techniques are what make tea different than herbs, spices, and other things people mix with water.

PLUCKING

As its name suggests, plucking is the process used to extract leaves from the tea plant. The way a person plucks the leaves plays an important role in the taste and aromas of the resulting tea. At its most simple, plucking triggers a tea bush to produce a sweet sap (a collection of chemicals that are responsible for the unique taste and aroma of tea). The more sap a tea farmer can create in his tea bushes, the more sweetness the leaves can produce and the more sweet his tea will taste.

Once the tea production begins, the plants will be plucked continuously for most of the year. This is done not only to gather more leaves but also to prohibit the tea plants from flowering. As soon as tea plants flower, they direct their energy toward sustaining the flower, forcing the leaves to go into hibernation, a stage in which the leaves become tough and brittle. If a bush or tree is plucked too aggressively, however, the tea farmer can severely damage the plant or kill it. A tea farmer must balance his needs for promoting sweeter teas with the plant's need for growth.

Most gardens "table" their plants, pruning them to grow no higher than shoulder height. Keeping the plants pruned in this manner makes it easier to pluck the leaves. It also creates stunning landscapes of perfectly trimmed rows of undulating tea bushes growing on the sides of mountains. This style of growing is relatively recent and was introduced by Buddhist monasteries that immaculately maintained their tea gardens to symbolize the belief that tea is a gift of life and should be honored. Today, farmers find it easier to tend to bushes kept in this manner because it is the most efficient way for pluckers to pluck the tea leaves. Prior to this more modern style of horticulture, farmers would leave the tea plants growing "wild"; that is, untrimmed and grown not in the shape of a bush but in the shape of a tree. You can still find teas made from the leaves of wild tea plants, but these teas are usually sold at a premium price because it takes more time to pluck the leaves and because people believe that having tea from a "natural" or "wild" tea plant is better than a tea made from the controlled growth of the contemporary tea gardens.

WITHERING

Another important process for creating high-quality tea is the process of withering. Withering helps create the myriad of tea's shapes, it initiates many of the important chemical changes that take place during the processing of tea, and it is one of the processes responsible for creating color, taste, and aroma. Virtually all teas are withered, even if it is just for the twenty to thirty minutes that a plucked leaf spends between being plucked and being transported into the production facility. Even so, not all teas are withered the same!

There are two distinct withering processes, and both play an important role not only in creating complex tastes and aromas but also in determining what type of tea is being made. These processes are colloquially referred to as physical withering and chemical withering.

PHYSICAL WITHERING

Physical withering reduces the moisture content of the leaf and makes the leaf pliable so that it is easier to manipulate in subsequent processes. All teas go through at least some physical withering. Without at least a little physical withering, it would be very difficult for a tea master to create the beautiful and distinctive shapes of tea.

CHEMICAL WITHERING

Chemical withering, on the other hand, is a more time-consuming process and facilitates the breakdown of the complex chemicals in a leaf's cells, changing these complex chemicals into simpler chemicals that add body and flavor to a tea. If allowed, chemical withering can start the oxidation process. Depending on the type of tea being processed, the tea master may limit the amount of chemical withering a leaf undergoes to create the desired taste and aroma profile. Or, as in the case of most of the unoxidized teas, he may avoid such processing altogether.

RUPTURING/ROLLING

Oolong and black tea are unique from the other types of tea because they both undergo a process in which the leaf's cell structure is ruptured.

By rupturing the cell walls of the tea leaf, known as rupturing or rolling, the tea master introduces oxygen to the polyphenol oxidase enzyme (PPO enzyme) and initiates the oxidation process (see "Oxidation" on page 59 for a more detailed discussion of the oxidation process).

Traditionally, the rolling process was conducted by rubbing leaves together between someone's hands. Today, in addition to the hand-rolling technique, rolling machines are most often used to replicate the hand-rolling process. Because black tea and oolong tea have different rates or percentage of oxidation, they utilize different machinery. But, the principles for each machine are the same and both mimic the traditional hand-rolling traditions.

In the 1930s, William McKercher invented a new process for making black tea, known as the cut, tear, and curl (CTC) process. A CTC machine is designed so that a withered tea leaf passes between two rollers with large teeth. These teeth cut and tear the leaf while the rollers crush and curl the leaves as they pass through. This not only gives the unique shape to CTC tea, but it also accelerates the oxidation process and drastically decreases the time it takes to process a black tea. It also creates a more bitter and full-bodied black tea that quickly turns liquid brown upon contact with water. Thus, it is the ideal process for high-volume, low-quality black tea. In fact, CTC processed tea constitutes a large percentage of the black tea sold in tea bags in the North American market today.

SHAQING

FIRING/DEACTIVATING PPO ENZYME

Almost all types of tea undergo some sort of firing in which the leaves are heated to deactivate the enzyme responsible for oxidation. This is known as the shaqing or kill-green process. There are many ways to fire a leaf, but the process usually consists of exposing the leaves to temperatures above 185°F (85°C) for anywhere between thirty seconds and five minutes. The shaqing process has a profound effect on how a tea tastes and smells. In some ways, this process is the hallmark of tea production.

Because leaves come in many sizes and shapes, the shaqing temperatures and processes are not the same for all teas. For example, oolong tea is often fired at extremely high temperatures, sometimes as high as 400°F–500°F (204°C–260°C), and tossed in a revolving drum for anywhere between one to five minutes. Also, many black teas and most dark teas do not undergo any shaqing at all because the oxidation process for these teas is halted during the drying stage.

DRYING

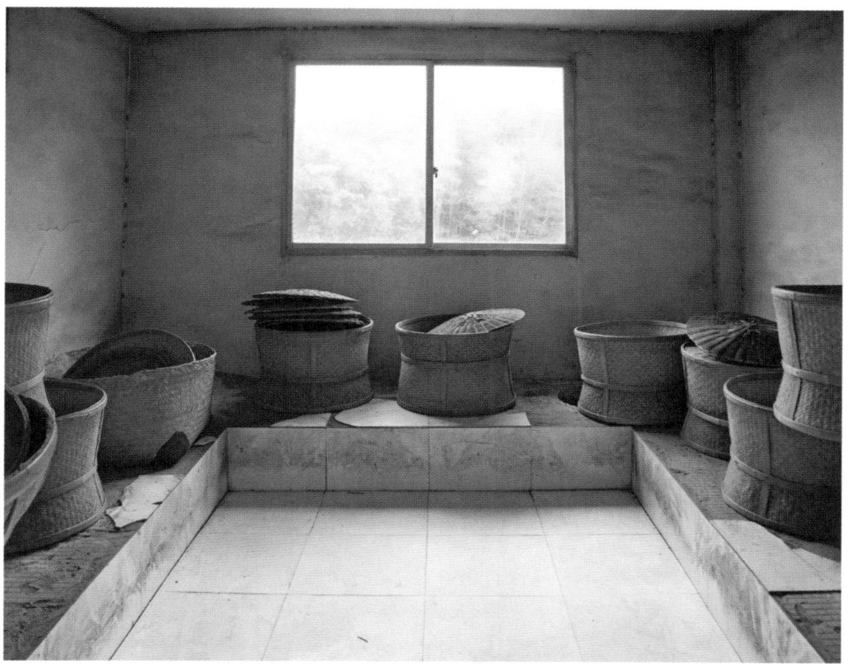

All teas go through a drying process in which the moisture content of the leaf is decreased to below 4–5 percent. Drying not only stops any enzymatic reactions (oxidation process), but it also removes moisture from the leaf so that the leaf is "shelf stable."

Over the past forty to fifty years, tea producers have discovered that although it is easy to accelerate the drying process with ovens, dehydrating tea too quickly leads to poor-tasting teas. Therefore, the process of drying has become a science, and teas are now uniformly dried at a rate in which a leaf loses between 2.8 and 3.6 percent of its moisture per hour until the total content is reduced to below the requisite 4–5 percent.

CRAFT

The competency or mastery of the person processing the tea plays a fundamentally important role in the taste, aroma, and appearance of a tea. As discussed later in the book, merely halting the oxidation process too late or too early dramatically alters the quality and taste of a tea. Interestingly, knowing when to halt this oxidation process is more an art than a science because it is often determined merely by smelling the aromas produced during the oxidation process. When the tea master smells the aroma he seeks, he will expose the leaves to immense heat to stop the oxidation process. The competency of a tea master goes a long way in determining whether these teas will have a pleasant taste and aroma.

Although a tea leaf's moisture content and size vary greatly from region to region, it is generally agreed that for every 220 pounds (100 kg) of leaves plucked, a tea master can produce anywhere between 33 and 55 pounds (15 and 25 kg) of dried tea.

VARIETIES AND CULTIVARS

A cultivar is a plant selected for its desirable characteristics and then subsequently maintained through propagation. It is horticulture's version of selective breeding.

The type of cultivar used in creating a tea plays a significant role in how a tea tastes, smells, and looks. Although it is common in the tea industry to hear people state that all tea comes from one plant, Camellia sinensis, this is a little deceptive. As explained in the history section, all tea might be from the same species, *C. sinensis*, but not all tea comes from the same variety. In fact, most of the giant industrial farms growing tea in the old colonial states such as India, Indonesia, Kenya, Sri Lanka, and so on, use *C. sinensis* var. *assamica*, not the older, more traditional *C. sinensis* var. *sinensis*. Taste a well-crafted Assam from India made with leaves from *C. sinensis* var. *assamica* and compare it to a black tea from China's Fujian Province made with leaves from *C. sinensis* var. *sinensis* and you will instantly taste the difference between these two varieties. The leaf of the assamica variety is much larger than its sinensis cousin; it tastes bitter and has more astringency. In fact, put a leaf from each variety under a microscope and you will notice that the teas do not just taste different—they have a different chemical composition.

Further, even within the same variety of *C. sinensis* all teas are not created equal. One of the most beautiful aspects of the Chinese and Japanese tea industries is the fact that over the past several millennia, villages have cultivated tea plants suitable to their unique processing techniques and subjective taste preferences, creating a plethora of cultivars, each with their own unique qualities. The thousands of cultivars cultivated over these millennia have created a patchwork of styles, tastes, and flavors.

What is more, specific types of teas are not always made from the same cultivar. It is common for different producers and different regions to use different cultivars for production of the same type of tea. For instance, in Japan there have been more than thirty cultivars officially registered in Japan for the production of Sencha green tea alone. Each cultivar creates its own unique flavor, aroma, and appearance. The different cultivars used in these regions are an important reason why these teas taste so different.

TYPES OF TEA

Of the various varieties of tea, green tea is the variety with the longest history and the most diversity in taste, aroma, and appearance. The difference in the taste of green tea is determined by the cultivar used, the soil in which it was grown, and the environmental conditions with which it grew. Most importantly, the taste and aroma of a green tea is affected by the mechanical processes the tea master uses in fixing the leaves' oxidizing enzyme and in drying the leaves. That is to say, the shaqing process used in processing the green tea is fundamentally important in determining the characteristics of that tea.

GREEN TEA

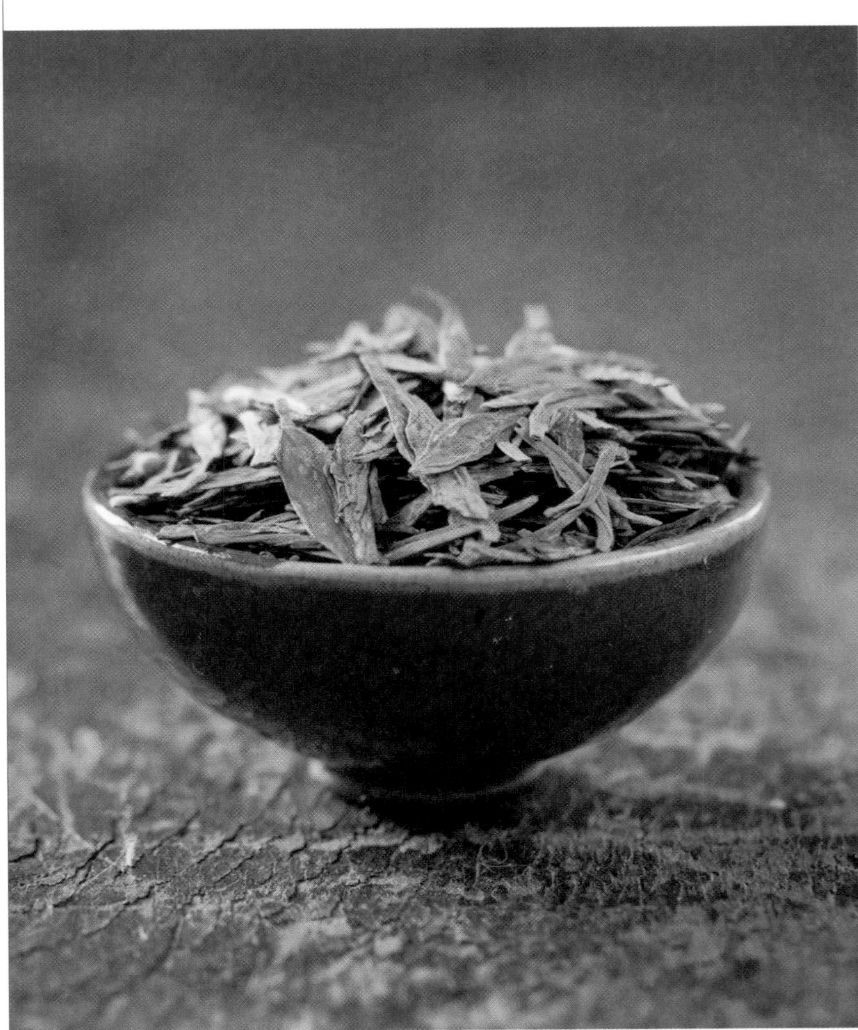

SHAQING

Most green teas go through a process of physical withering (see "Processing" for a more thorough discussion of mechanical withering). After the leaves are withered and are pliable enough to be shaped and formed, the tea master introduces heat to the leaf to deactivate or "kill" the PPO enzyme (the enzyme responsible for oxidizing the tea leaf). For the production of green tea, a tea master chooses between four processes. That is to say, there are four ways one can use to neutralize the PPO enzyme in a tea leaf, to stop the leaves from oxidizing, and to make a green tea: steaming, baking, sun drying, and pan frying.

STEAMING

Steaming tea leaves is a traditional Chinese shaqing method. Coincidentally, this traditional Chinese method is now rarely used in China, whereas it is the primary method of fixing the oxidizing enzyme in Japanese green teas. This is especially interesting considering that it is believed the Japanese did not attempt steaming tea until around the middle of the eighteenth century. Steaming tea leaves creates a characteristic "grassy" taste and aroma as well as the bright green color associated with many of the Japanese green teas. A grassy-tasting tea is often described as tasting "green." Indeed, it is hard not to describe a steamed green tea as tasting "green." Some of the most well-known and revered steamed green teas are the Japanese green teas Gyokuro and Sencha.

BAKING

Baking tea leaves is similar to how one would bake a loaf of bread—in a large oven. As such, baked teas are often associated with mass-processed, low-quality green tea. This association makes sense not only because it is very economical to bake large quantities of tea leaves, especially when using large automated ovens, but also because the automation process creates tea leaves that lack a certain freshness, subtle taste, and complex aroma.

Although baked teas are often associated with lower-quality teas, there are highly regarded teas that still use the baking method for shaqing. The difference between these highly regarded teas and the commodity teas is that the lower-graded, commodity tea undergoes an automated process of baking that cannot create the subtle flavors and aromas required to be graded as a quality tea. To bake a tea and still achieve a complex and nuanced taste, a tea is generally quick-baked to around 350°F (177°C) to neutralize the PPO enzyme.

Once the PPO enzyme is destroyed or neutralized and the oxidation halted, the tea master repeats a series of steps in which he alternates between shaping, baking, and cooling the leaves until the desired shape, taste, and aroma is achieved. Some of the most regarded green teas that undergo such a baking process are Liu An Gua Pian and Taiping Houkui.

SUN DRYING

As the name suggests, under the sun-drying method, leaves are laid on mats in partial sun and allowed to dry. While lying in the sun, the leaves are tossed or shaken so that they dry uniformly. After the leaves lose approximately 60 percent of their original moisture content, they are finish-fired and sorted. This very old method of neutralizing the PPO enzyme is used today primarily to make dark teas (see "Dark Tea" for more discussion).

DRYING

Finally, after the PPO enzyme has been destroyed, all green tea leaves are dried. Today, most green teas are dried in ovens. In China, you can still find many of the higher-graded green teas dried in wicker air driers, in which warm air circulates around the leaves as they sit in wicker baskets. This process allows the leaves to retain their natural sweetness but is very time consuming. The leaves are warmed for just minutes at a time and are then left to cool. This process of drying and cooling is repeated until the leaves' water content is below 5 percent.

Because baking tea leaves creates an economical yet shallow-tasting tea, this process is used for much of the world's scented green teas, such as jasmine tea. The scenting hides the qualities of the base green tea, allowing processors to create large quantities of tea in which the quality of the base green tea is irrelevant. Plus, because they use low-grade green tea they can sell it at a much larger profit, especially because it is easy to market a tea that smells as lovely as fresh jasmine flowers.

PAN FRYING

Pan frying is traditionally done by hand on a wok over an open flame. Today, pan frying green tea by hand is done only for the highest-graded teas. The other pan-fried teas are fried in a heated revolving drum or other proprietary equipment that rolls the teas while simultaneously frying them. When done with proper care and skill, the contact between the leaves and the hot metal triggers the Maillard reaction, a reaction that occurs when the leaves reach a certain temperature allowing their proteins and sugars to react with their amino acids to form molecules that create unique odors and flavors. In more simple terms, the Maillard reaction creates teas with a unique roasted nut taste.

Perhaps the most revered of all pan-fried green tea is Dragonwell (Longjing). Whether this tea gained fame because of its proximity to the megacities of Shanghai and Hangzhou or because it truly is the smoothest and sweetest green tea is hard to know. What is not difficult to understand is the fact that once you taste a quality Dragonwell tea, it will capture your heart with its naturally sweet and nutty flavors.

Also incorrectly known as browning, the Maillard reaction (pronounced May-ard) is most often associated with the unique flavors and aromas of steak, coffee, caramel, and toast. The Maillard reaction is a non-enzymatic browning caused by the condensation of an amino group and a reducing compound that results in complex changes in a food's aroma, flavor, and color. This reaction is extremely important in the creation of certain tea's desirable sweetness and nuttiness. But, controlling the reaction to create a uniform-tasting tea is extremely difficult. Chemists at the University of British Columbia estimate that it may require the generation of one hundred to two hundred individual chemicals in the proper concentration and ratio to form one specific flavor in tea. Furthermore, the individual chemicals released during the Maillard reaction are contingent on a very specific ratio of a leaf's pH level, its water content, its temperature, and surrounding environmental variables such as humidity. This complexity is why tea masters are so revered throughout the tea world and why it takes a lifetime of learning to understand how to recreate tastes, aromas, and color while pan-frying handmade teas.

As with all of China's history, there are many myths surrounding the origins of China's teas. Dragonwell is no exception. This tea takes its name from a natural well located outside Hangzhou. It is told that, because this well allegedly never dries, even in the worst of droughts, Emperor Qianlong of the Qing dynasty, who apparently enjoyed traveling to the Shanghai and Hangzhou basin, inscribed the Chinese characters "Long Jing," or Dragon Well, above the well to commemorate its importance to the area. The connection between the natural well, Emperor Qianlong, and Dragonwell tea is not clear or consistent. Regardless, it is universally agreed that Longjing made from the waters of this well is one of the finest pleasures to be experienced in all of life. Dragonwell is traditionally evaluated based on "four perfections," or the four characteristics unique to a quality Dragonwell. Perhaps not informative on their own, these four perfections are jade color, sweet smell, mellow flavor, and pleasing shape. Admittedly poetic in description, these four perfections have generally been ignored in favor of more practical concerns such as location of the tea garden, date of harvest, and tenderness of the leaves.

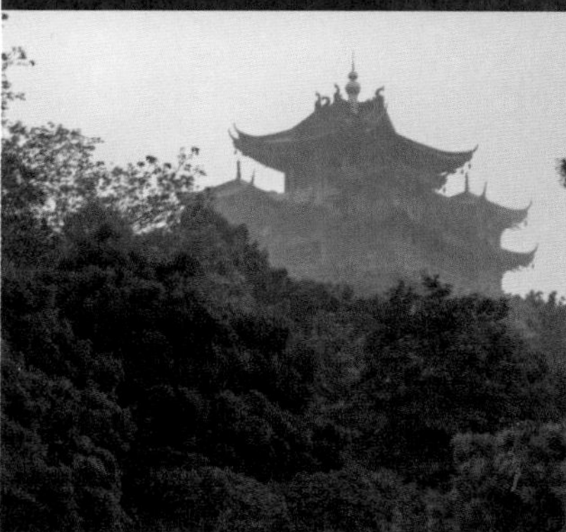

Although most Japanese green teas today are steamed, the Japanese produce a very unique panfried green tea called Hojicha. This brown-in-color green tea was created sometime in the early nineteenth century when tea merchants began roasting low-grade tea leaves over charcoal (this process has been modernized, with most Hojicha manufacturers now using drum roasters, similar to what coffee roasters use in their roasting production). Hojicha's roasting process creates an intense nutty and caramel taste and aroma, as well as distinctive red leaves. The leaves used for this tea are picked late in the season and are rarely sorted. Therefore, Hojicha contains a lot of non-leaf matter, providing a lower caffeine level than most teas. The Japanese often think of Hojicha as a later afternoon/evening tea and will use it as the tea in which they introduce their children into the pleasures of drinking tea.

WHITE TEA

Compared to other types of tea, white tea as it is known today is an extremely modern invention. Developed in the Fuding prefecture of the Fujian Province in southeast China, it is believed that white teas have been processed for only the past two hundred years. White tea gets its name not from the light liquor that it creates, but from the silvery pekoe (hairs or dust) that grow on the unopened buds of a tea leaf. Because today's white tea is so young, there are not nearly as many varieties on the market as green or oolong tea, making it one of the more approachable and easy-to-understand types of tea.

PROCESSING

White tea generally has the least amount of processing of the six types of tea. In fact, after plucking, white tea undergoes only two processing steps: withering and drying. Traditionally, white tea leaves were laid in direct sun or under a canopy in a way that allowed the ambient air to waft over the leaves to wither and dry them. Unlike most green teas, white tea undergoes a substantial amount of physical withering with some processers allowing the leaves to wither for days.

After the teas are withered (some until their water content falls below 10 percent), they are dried. Each white tea–producing region uses different techniques for drying the leaves. Most have created proprietary techniques for placing the withered leaves on some sort of platform over which they blow extremely warm air. Such systems allow not only for accelerated drying but also uniformity in the drying. Many processors are increasingly using ovens to dry the leaves. Ovens allow for more consistent drying and more control as to how quickly the leaves will dry.

TYPES

The three classic Chinese white teas are Yinzhen (Silver Needle), Bai Mu Dan, and Shou Mei. Although white tea is not "graded" per se, it is still helpful to think of grades when understanding the three types of white tea. Silver Needle represents the highest graded white tea and should consist of only the unopened bud of the Da Bai cultivar. Bai Mu Dan can then be thought of as the middle graded white tea because it consists of the bud and first two leaves of the pluck. Shou Mei can be thought of as the lowest graded Chinese white tea. As other regions around the world start producing white tea, it is becoming more difficult to know the caliber of these non-Chinese white teas without tasting and examining the leaves, because each new region creating white teas is adopting its own nomenclature to name its new teas.

One of the common misconceptions about white tea is that it is the least oxidized of all types of tea. A lot of white tea, especially Shou Mei, undergoes substantial heap withering, in which the leaves sit in a big heap and wither for long periods of time. This process breaks down the cellular structure of the leaves and often begins the oxidation process. It is common for tea producers to slightly oxidize their white teas, especially for their lower-graded white teas, with some teas receiving up to 5–6 percent or even 10 percent oxidation.

Within the category of Silver Needle tea (Yinzhen in Chinese) there are some distinctions worth noting. The highest graded Silver Needle tea is labeled White Hair Silver Needle (Baihao Yinzhen in Chinese). Because this tea is made with only the top bud set, it is not only considered the best grade of Silver Needle teas, but it is also the most prized and, therefore, the most expensive. If you discover a company advertising Baihao Yinzhen or White Hair Silver Needle and the cost doesn't make you gasp, it is probably misclassified. These distinctions are merely illustrative, because there are other white teas that stand outside the classic triumvirate of Fujian white teas. For instance, Mo Xiao Yu Ya is a highly regarded white tea that is very difficult to find outside of China. But, having a good grasp of these three white teas gets you most of the way toward understanding white tea.

Although a genuine Silver Needle tea should be made from the Da Bai cultivar, not all Da Bai cultivars are created equal. Separated only by a line on the map, the northernmost counties of Zhenghe and Fuding in China's southern Fujian Province have each produced its own unique Da Bai cultivars: the Zhenghe Da Bai cultivar and the Fuding Da Bai cultivar. These cultivars, in turn, have led to the creation of two unique styles for Silver Needle: the Zhenghe style, which is thought to have a fuller body due to the Zhenghe villages' tradition of allowing the leaves to wilt in a pile for long periods of time, and the Fuding style, which has a lighter taste because the leaves are generally not allowed to sit in a pile.

Shou Mei is unique because it consists of only the more mature leaves of the pluck and is picked later in the season. Many describe Shou Mei as having a unique aroma and a floral taste similar to lightly oxidized oolong teas. The best explanation for this commonly held idea is that both teas are picked later during the harvest, and Shou Mei is withered for so long that it is often allowed to undergo a bit of oxidation, much like lightly oxidized oolong teas.

Although Shou Mei has historically been a "peasant" tea, as interest in tea increases throughout the world, tea companies are beginning to introduce it as a unique specialty tea. Further, because Shou Mei is traditionally sold to peasants at very low cost, tea producers have large quantities from past tea harvests in their warehouses. It is now common to see tea companies highlight the year of a Shou Mei's harvest, as if it improves with age like a wine. Certainly Shou Mei's flavor and aroma change over time. Whether those changes should be considered an improvement is best left to you and your own preferences.

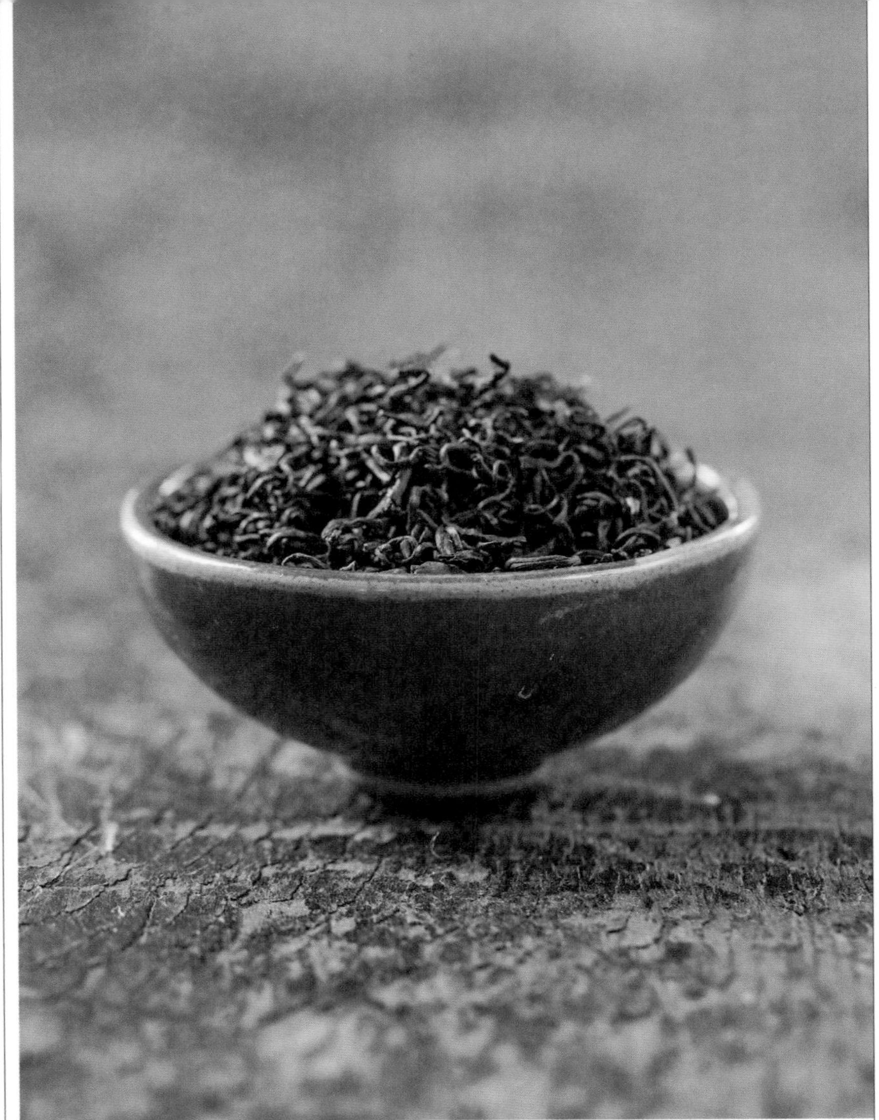

BLACK TEA

The basic processes used during the production of all black teas are withering, rolling, oxidization, and drying. Black tea is an outlier from other forms of tea because of the large presence of condensed catechins (i.e., polyphenols formed during oxidation). This is an impressive way of saying that black tea is unique in the tea world because it goes through a significant oxidation process.

OXIDATION

The flavor of a black tea is determined, in part, by the length and time of oxidation. There is very much an art to crafting a black tea because the flavor profile develops quickly during the oxidation process, but at some point the sought-after flavor quickly begins to disappear.

There are six unique factors that influence how a leaf oxidizes and, therefore, there are six factors that influence how a black tea tastes.

First, although it is generally agreed that the prime temperature for triggering the oxidation of a black tea is around 84°F (29°C), any fluctuation in this temperature greatly influences the amount of moisture the leaf loses as well as the amount and type of catechins that are oxidized.

Second, the consistency and strength of the withering affects how a leaf oxidizes. If the leaves were unevenly withered or withered too quickly, then the leaf's catechins will oxidize differently and the taste of the tea will change.

Third, the size and subtleness of a leaf affects the time it takes for a leaf's catechins to react with oxygen.

Fourth, intermingling different cultivars or leaves plucked from different areas can lead to uneven oxidation because different leaves will have different capacities for oxidation. They might be different sizes or they might have grown in different conditions (e.g., one grown in full sun, whereas others grown in partial sun). Such uneven oxidation creates uneven taste and quality.

Fifth, when a tea master oxidizes a tea leaf, he must evaluate four distinct taste characteristics: briskness, brightness, astringency, and strength. Each of these characteristics emerges and then disappears at different stages of the oxidation process. The tea master must therefore determine which of these characteristics takes precedence while trying to balance all four characteristics present in a black tea.

Sixth, the environmental conditions in which the oxidation takes place can have a great effect on the consistency of the overall oxidation. The amount of oxygen present, room temperature, breezes, and other types of contaminants affect the overall quality of oxidation.

OTHER VARIABLES AFFECTING TASTE OF BLACK TEA

The quality and taste of a black tea is also determined by the amount of soluble matter in the leaf (chemicals that dissolve during different tea processing stages). This is especially true in black tea because soluble matter in the leaf will transform during the oxidation process. This transformation creates unique tastes and aromas. The soluble matter in any given tea leaf is a by-product of not only the type of cultivar used but also the land in which the leaf grew. Not only does each cultivar contain different levels of soluble matter, but the same cultivars grown in different regions also will contain different levels of soluble matter.

EVALUATING BLACK TEA

One of the hallmarks of evaluating the quality of a black tea is by assessing how tightly the leaves are rolled. Generally, higher-graded teas are teas with leaves that are tightly and uniformly rolled. Lower-graded teas, on the other hand, are teas with leaves that are loosely and inconsistently rolled. With that said, the tightness of the roll has more to do with the steepability of a leaf than it does with the taste of a tea. Therefore, one should not evaluate the tea's drinkability or taste merely because its leaves are not tightly rolled. It is common to find that people prefer the taste of looser rolled black teas over more expensive or more highly graded black teas that have been tightly rolled.

SOUTH ASIAN CLASSIFICATION

In the twentieth century, commodity black tea from India took over virtually the entire tea market. Grading black teas has therefore become confusing, with industry jargon that is understood only by those trading in one of the world's tea auction houses.

The English/Indian system of grading tea is based on a hierarchy of words that relate to visual characteristics of the tea leaves. The first letter of each of these words is strung together to create an acronym. It is through these various acronyms that a tea's grade is designated. The grades are evaluated based on the benchmark "orange pekoe" (OP). Any acronym above the OP grade is considered a higher-quality tea, and teas that are labeled with an acronym found below the OP grade are deemed to be lower-quality teas. Making the entire system unapproachable to all but a very few is the fact that the benchmark grade OP has nothing to do with the flavor or color of the tea even though the word orange is used. Rather, orange pekoe simply denotes a black tea consisting of whole leaves (not dust or fannings) but no "tippiness" (i.e., orange-colored leaves).

Although most tea auctions have closed in the old colonial territories, this system still endures. How or why the system still exists is a topic about which I cannot speculate. Simply look at the hierarchy under this old system and you will instantly recognize that its attributes do not lie in its ease of use:

SFTGFOP-1: Super Fine Tippy Golden Flowery Orange Pekoe—Grade 1

SFTGFOP: Super Fine Tippy Golden Flowery Orange Pekoe

FTGFOP: Fine Tippy Golden Flowery Orange Pekoe

TGFOP: Tippy Golden Flowery Orange Pekoe

GFOP: Golden Flowery Orange Pekoe

FOP: Flowery Orange Pekoe

OP: Orange Pekoe (benchmark)

BOP: Broken Orange Pekoe

FBOP: Flowery Broken Orange Pekoe

TGBOP: Tippy Golden Broken Orange Pekoe

BOPF: Broken Orange Pekoe Fannings

BOPD: Broken Orange Pekoe Dust

OOLONG TEA

Leaves for oolong tea are picked throughout the entire year and constitute a large percentage of the specialty teas plucked later in the growing seasons. By allowing the leaves to stay on the tea plants longer, the tea master allows the leaves to acquire chemicals not present when the leaves first bud. These chemicals, along with the complex production process, create the unique taste and aromas of many of the oolong teas.

PROCESSING

After the leaves are plucked, they are withered in the sun for a relatively short period of time (between one and four hours) and then allowed to cool in a damp room. This short withering process generally is repeated three times. After this series of withering, the leaves usually undergo a "sweating" stage. In this stage, the leaves are gently but continuously tossed in a room with temperatures maintained at 68°F–84°F (20°C–29°C) and a humidity rate of over 80 percent. The continuous tossing allows the leaves to dry evenly while also helping to rupture their cellular structure. Once the cellular structure is ruptured, the atmospheric oxygen begins to mix with the leaves' PPO enzyme and the leaves begin to oxidize. Unlike black teas, which have very even oxidation because the oxidation occurs while the leaves are subjected to the extreme stress and pressure of rolling, oolong's oxidation process does not always occur evenly. During the sweating stage, the oxidation begins on the outside of the leaf and slowly works itself toward the center. This usually results in the creation of a beautiful red ring around the edge of the leaves. Today's oolongs, with market pressures requiring uniform-looking leaves, rarely contain this unique red ring. Today's tea processors use various techniques to accelerate the oxidation process. One of the by-products of these new techniques is that the leaves are more uniformly oxidized and the distinctive red bands are usually absent.

After the sweating stage, the leaves are cooled and then shaped. All oolong teas come in one of two shapes: the traditional style with long curvy leaves, and the contemporary style of "wrap curling" where the leaves are rolled into small beads with a tail. To form oolong in the traditional style, the leaves are tossed until they are sufficiently rolled. To form oolong in the contemporary style, often associated with Fujian's Tie Guan Yin, the tea master wraps the tossed leaves in a cloth and places the wrap in a mold that he uses to roll the leaves into their unique "bead with tail" shape.

OXIDATION

Creating tea is an art. This is especially true with the creation of oolong tea. Oolongs are considered "partially oxidized" tea and the amount of oxidation for each oolong varies greatly. Some oolongs are oxidized as little as 6–8 percent, whereas others are oxidized more than 85 percent. It is the responsibility of the tea master to determine when to stop the oxidation. He does this simply by smelling the various aromas created during oxidation and by observing the shape of the leaves while being processed. When the aroma is to his satisfaction and the leaves are suitably shaped, he halts the oxidation process by exposing the leaves to very high temperatures (392°F–500°F, or 200°C–260°C) to destroy the PPO enzyme. Because the leaves are exposed to such high temperatures, this stage lasts only minutes. The extreme heat destroys the PPO enzyme, stops the enzymatic oxidation, and makes the leaves very pliable. If the tea master stops the oxidation too early or too late, he will create an altogether different-tasting tea.

After the oxidation process, many Oolongs are roasted over charcoal. This process not only produces a "masculine," roasted, tar-like taste, it provides a much longer shelf life for the tea. That is to say, the more roast the leaves receive, the longer they will last. The downside of heavily roasting the leaves is that the char taste can become so pungent that one must let the tea sit for up to a year to allow the taste to mellow and to provide a good tasting tea.

Da Hong Pao is a Chinese national treasure. Today you can still visit the three mother bushes from which Da Hong Pao was allegedly originally created. As with all great Chinese legends, the legend of Da Hong Pao is pure fantasy and is never told the same way twice. It has been said that nine dragons ravaged the area that is now called Wuyishan (rock mountains) in the northern section of China's Fujian Province. To quash the chaos, a god destroyed the dragons, turning their corpses into black rock cliffs. In commemoration of his heroic feat, the god planted tea bushes high on one of these cliffs so that no mortal could destroy them. While meditating, a monk noticed the bushes. Fortuitously, this monk was hiding a monkey in his robe.

Because monkeys cannot harm a tree's spirit and are, therefore, capable of pulling leaves from divine tea bushes, the monk directed his monkey to climb the cliff and pick the most-tender leaves from the bushes. Even more fantastical, the monk was associated with a monastery in which a scholar was suffering from severe stomach ailments, making it impossible for the scholar to bring honor and wealth to his family and village. The monk steeped the divine leaves and served his tea to the sickly scholar. Voilà! The scholar was healed.

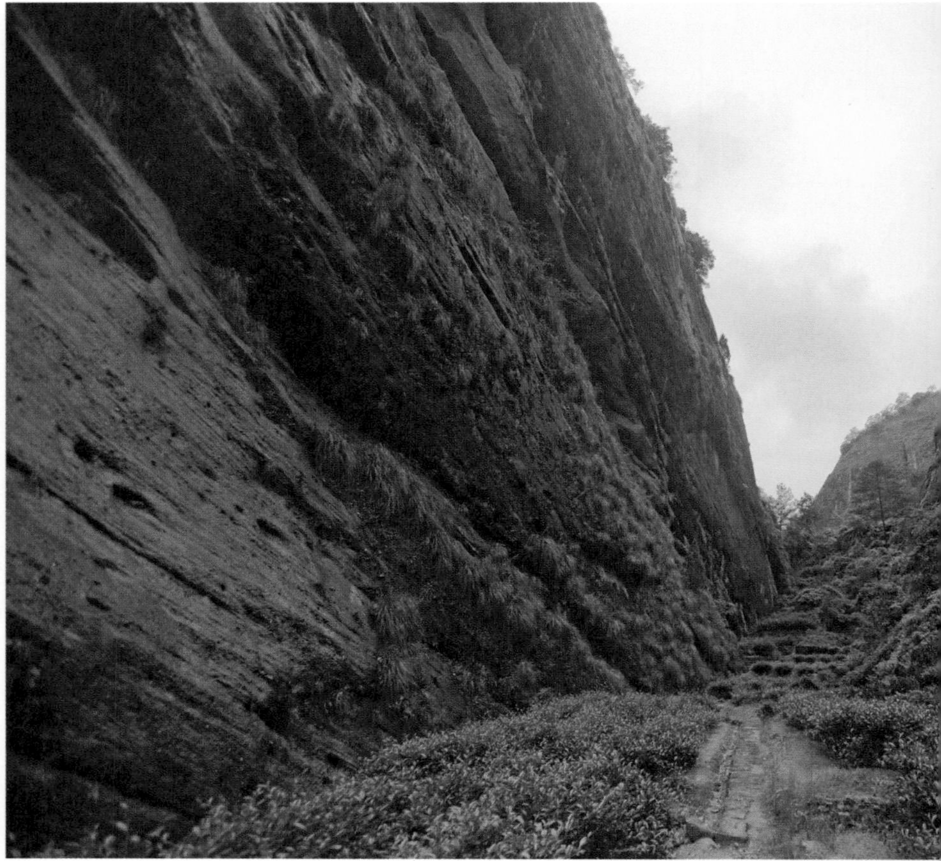

Regaining his strength, the scholar traveled north to sit for an Imperial test of knowledge. With his mind alive from the divine tea, the scholar mastered the exams and was asked to meet with the emperor. At this meeting, the scholar discovered that the emperor suffered from the very same ailments as he did. So, he brewed his tea and healed the emperor. The emperor requested that the scholar return every harvest with the leaves from the first picking of his newly discovered tea plants and gave the scholar a large red cloth to protect the young leaves. Thus, the legend of Da Hong Pao (big red robe) was born. The story of the Da Hong Pao is so endearing that teas made from the remaining trees are protected by armed guards and produce teas that are unsurpassed in price (one ounce of Da Hong Pao can fetch thousands of dollars).

DRYING AND SHAPING

Once the oxidation has been halted, the leaves are dried. Today, most oolongs are dried in ovens in one step. Some high-graded oolong teas, especially WuYi oolongs, still undergo several drying stages during which each subsequent stage dries the leaves in increasingly cooler temperatures. By gently cooling the oolong tea in this manner, the tea acquires a unique toasty flavor, a hallmark of the WuYi oolongs.

The undisputed kings of oolongs are the WuYi oolongs (rock oolongs) from the area surrounding the city of Wuyishan in the northern part of the Fujian Province. These teas get their name from the grand rock mountains between which the plants grow. Of the rock oolongs, Da Hong Pao (big red robe) is the king among kings. Over the years, Da Hong Pao has been the subject of many myths and legends. Fortunately (or unfortunately), today's Da Hong Pao teas are only an approximation of the original. Traditionally, Da Hong Pao was more thoroughly oxidized than today's version and the tea underwent numerous dry roasting stages. Today, very few iterations of Da Hong Pao are dry roasted and are generally less oxidized than the more traditional version, giving today's Da Hong Pao a more floral aroma and flavor. Other notable rock oolongs are Shui Jin Gui (golden water turtle), Tie Luo Han (iron arhat or iron warrior monk), and the very rare Bai Ji Guan (white cocksomb).

TAIWANESE OOLONG

Taiwan has processed tea since the early 1700s and has produced oolong tea for approximately 150 years. Today, the small Taiwanese islands supply roughly 20 percent of the world's oolong teas.

Taiwan can be divided into five distinct growing regions: northern Taiwan, midcentral Taiwan, eastern Taiwan, south-central Taiwan, and high mountain. Of particular note, the midcentral region produces teas mostly from cultivars brought over from China's Fujian Province, which is located on the western side of the Taiwan Strait.

Perhaps the most famous Taiwanese tea from this region is an oolong tea named Dong Ding. Dong Ding also happens to be the most closely related to many of the famous oolong teas growing in the northern section of the Fujian province. It has had the most influence on reducing the oxidation levels and changing the taste and aroma profiles for many of China's classic teas, especially Tie Guan Yin, over the last one hundred years.

China's cultural revolution left an indelible mark on the world's tea market. Historically, Taiwanese oolongs could not compete with the mainland Chinese oolongs. When trade between the West and China essentially stopped in the 1900s, the oolong market was supported almost exclusively by the farms in Taiwan, most of which were producing teas only for the domestic Taiwanese market. Over the past 80 years, as tea drinkers were exposed almost exclusively to Taiwanese oolongs, they adjusted their palates. Now the flavor profiles created from the oolongs grown and processed in Taiwan are dictating how the mainland processes its oolongs. The biggest change over the past one hundred years has been that Chinese processors are oxidizing their oolong teas significantly less than they traditionally did to create a more gentle, floral, and aromatic tea.

YELLOW TEA

Yellow tea originated in the Anhui and Hupei Provinces. Although it might be the smallest category of tea based on its production volume, there are written records showing that yellow tea may have been produced as early as the Tang dynasty (618–907).

Yellow tea is such a small category of tea that there is not even a consensus as to whether this category should exist. Some describe yellow tea as nothing more than a very high-quality green tea that is so pure in production, taste, and aroma that it is fit for a king. Others describe yellow tea as a tea that is made through a unique heap withering stage conducted after the tea is fired to deactivate the PPO enzyme. This heap withering stage triggers a non-enzymatic oxidation process—this is in contrast to white tea, which undergoes its heaping before the firing process. Whether such a category is warranted is not a discussion in which I am interested. More important to this book is the fact that for at least the past three hundred years, certain villages have created interesting proprietary techniques for processing tea leaves. These innovations, in turn, created very unique-looking and unique-tasting teas—teas that are now commonly referred to as yellow tea.

Technically, the distinguishing process for yellow tea is a series of heaping stages that allow the leaves to undergo a non-enzymatic oxidation process. This non-enzymatic oxidation process is how the leaves obtain their characteristic yellow appearance and floral taste.

Like green teas, yellow teas are fired to deactivate or kill the PPO enzyme and thus prohibit enzymatic oxidation. Virtually all yellow teas are made via the pan-frying method. Unlike panfried green teas, however, yellow teas start on a much cooler pan (203°F–221°F, or 95°C–105°C) and are slowly warmed (usually to approximately 266°F, or 130°C).

After leaves are heated enough to deactivate the PPO enzyme, the leaves undergo a smothering or heaping process in which the leaves are wrapped in cloth or paper, placed inside a pot, covered with a wet cloth, and left for days. Wrapping the leaves in this way creates a very humid environment, keeps the leaves surrounded by warm air, and prohibits the circulation of air. It is during this process that the leaves undergo their non-enzymatic oxidation process and in which the leaves begin to turn their characteristic yellow color. In fact, the wrapping process not only produces the teas' distinctive yellow leaves, it also creates a distinctive floral aroma and eliminates any unwanted bitterness in the leaves. This floral aroma and natural sweet taste is why many are content to simply call yellow tea a very high-quality green tea.

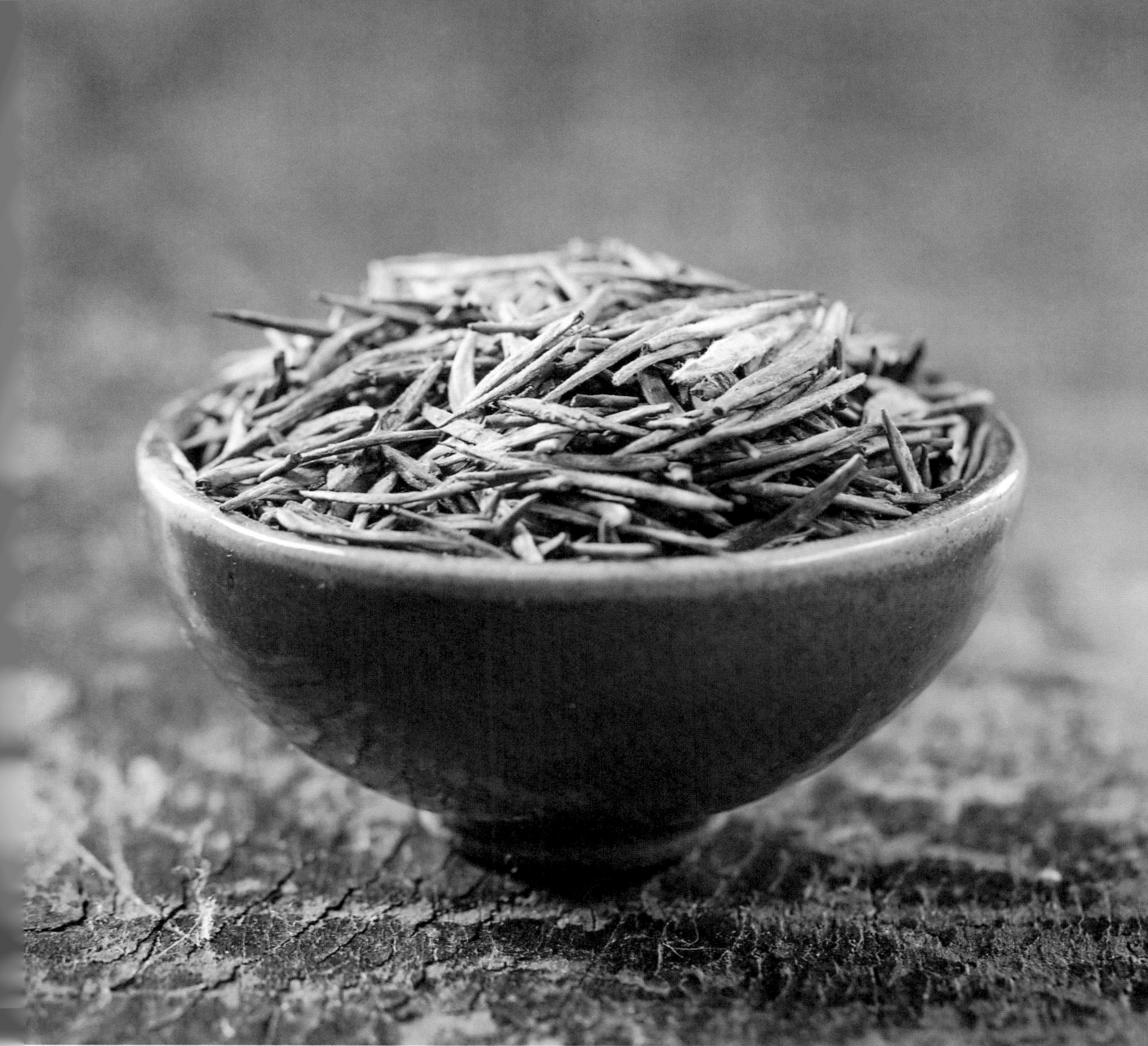

The leaves are then removed from their wrapping and undergo a second heating. This second heating decreases the leaves' moisture content and makes the water content uniform. The leaves are then wrapped again in cloth or paper and placed in a box. Like the first wrapping stage, this stage furthers the non-enzymatic oxidation and enhances the unique color, taste, and aroma of the yellow tea. Depending on the type of tea being crafted, these wrapping stages can vary dramatically. For instance, for the production of Bei Gang Mao Jian, the wrapping stage lasts just minutes, whereas for Wen Zhou Huang Tang it can last days. Regardless of the time the leaves are wrapped, after the second wrapping the leaves are roasted or baked until the moisture content drops below 5 percent. Unlike green and white teas, yellow teas are generally dried at lower temperatures and over a series of dryings with each subsequent drying done at a cooler temperature, similar to how many WuYi oolongs are dried.

DARK TEA

One of the most popular categories of tea and yet one of the most misunderstood tea categories is dark tea. This type of tea is often misunderstood as containing only Pu'erh tea. Although Pu'erh is a dark tea, it is not the only type of dark tea. As one of the oldest and most processed of all tea categories, the dark tea category trails only its green and oolong tea brethren in the amount of production dedicated to it.

One of the reasons why this type of tea is often confusing is the fact that dark tea is often referred to as "post-fermented" tea. Unfortunately, the term "post-fermented" is meaningless and, therefore, not helpful in understanding this tea's uniqueness. Dark tea is defined simply as a tea that undergoes a fermentation process. Nothing happens after, or "post," the fermentation process other than your enjoyment.

HISTORY

Dark tea is called *hei cha* in Chinese. The term *hei cha* did not originate until sometime during the Ming dynasty (1368–1644), but the precursor to *hei cha* or dark tea was processed in southwest China at least before the fourteenth century. Although there is no real consensus as to when dark tea originated, it is agreed that some sort of dark tea was being processed at least as early as the Sung dynasty (960–1279), if not as early as the Tang dynasty (618–907). During both the Sung and Tang dynasties, Sichuan was the crossroads for trade between China and the people in south and central Asia. Because these trade routes went through vast deserts and mountains, the traders did not have much access to plants and vegetables and their diets were reliant on meat. So, tea was essential. It not only provided essential vitamins and minerals, it also worked as a natural diuretic (the reason virtually all of China's minority groups in western and southwestern China exclusively drink dark tea still today). Lasting months, the teas' journey constantly exposed it to water and heat, perfect conditions for the activation of the yeast and fungus cells growing naturally on the tea leaves. With the yeast activated, the teas would start fermenting and the tea's taste, aroma, and appearance changed and mellowed.

Within the dark tea category of Pu'erh there are two types: Sheng Pu'erh and Shou Pu'erh. Shou Pu'erh is a dark tea generally made from the leaves of var. assamica. It is processed using the wodui method in which the leaves are heaped and exposed to heat and moisture until fermentation is triggered. Sheng Pu'erh, on the other hand, is made from a variety of cultivars grown in the Yunnan Province and does not use the *wodui* method. Instead, it is aged under controlled temperatures and humidity for at least three to five years. Some debate whether Sheng Pu'erh should even be considered a dark tea or whether it represents something altogether different.

Over the past fourteen hundred years, tea producers in southwest China began to replicate the conditions of these journeys by introducing heat and humidity into the leaves during the tea production process. This process was eventually refined until the Chinese developed the processing technique known today as *wodui*, a process very similar to a controlled composting.

PROCESSING

Dark teas undergo four distinct processing stages: shaqing (PPO enzyme deactivation), rolling/shaping, fermentation, and drying. Some dark teas are compressed into various shapes while others are sold loose. Whether loose or compressed, all dark teas follow these four steps.

FERMENTATION

Most important to the production of dark tea is the process of fermentation, a process in which various microbes, primarily various species of the Aspergillus mold, feed on chemicals in the tea leaves. During fermentation, a tea leaf's chemistry is altered, making it taste more mellow and less bitter.

Today, there are generally three techniques used to ferment tea: *wodui* (described above), pickling, and hybrid. As the name suggests, pickling is a process in which the tea master introduces natural lactic acid bacteria to very wet tea. After the fermentation process is completed, the tea is again dried. This process is similar to the eastern European process of making sauerkraut from cabbage, although the final tea is dried before selling. The third technique is a hybrid of the *wodui* method and pickling.

MOLD

Some compressed dark teas are charred over charcoal to "clean" the tea and to remove any fungus, mold, or bacteria that might alter the intended taste and aroma of the tea. Other dark teas, namely Hunan Fu Zhuan or Anhua Fu Brick tea, are notable because they are processed so that they actually enhance the growth of these molds. In fact, the quality of Hunan Fu Zhan is determined precisely by the amount of mold spores on the tea leaves. These "golden flowers" are said to have extremely beneficial health benefits. The more spores present on the tea, the higher quality it is considered.

To make Anhua Fu Zhuan, the tea leaf must be inoculated with the "golden flower" during the heaping process. This is done in one of three ways: the spores are dry mixed with a food such as rice flour, barley flour, or wheat flour and then mixed with the dry tea leaves and stems; the mold spores are mixed with a saline solution that is sprayed on the dry leaves and stems; or the mold spores are mixed directly with the dry leaves and stems. Once inoculated and within twenty-five hours of being exposed to the mold spores, the leaves and stems are placed in a fermentation chamber. The chamber's temperature is set at a very warm temperature of 90°F–113°F (32°C–45°C) for anywhere between five and one hundred hours.

Besides the very famous Yunnan Pu'erh dark tea, some of the other common Chinese dark teas are Fu Zhuan (Hunan), Lao Qing Ye (Hubei), Liu Bao (Guangxi), Nan Lu Bian (Sichuan), and Xi Lu Bian (Sichuan). Although much less common than the Chinese dark teas, other countries also ferment teas. For instance, Japan creates Awa Bancha (pickled) and Goishicha (hybrid), and Thailand produces a pickled tea called Miang Kham.

TERROIR

INTRODUCTION TO TERROIR

Borrowing from the wine industry and starting in the early twenty-first century, tea companies began introducing the concept of terroir into their discussions about tea.

As a concept, terroir expresses the way the geography, geology, and climate of a particular place affects the taste of that place's agricultural products. The wine industry beautifully utilizes this "sense of place" to differentiate wines made from the same grape but grown in different areas of the world. For instance, a wine connoisseur often differentiates between the earthy and chalky pinot noir wines of France's Burgundy region and the fruitier pinot noirs of the Napa Valley region in the United States. The difference in these two distinct pinot noir wines, both made from the same grapes, is a result of each region's unique geology, geography, and climate; it is a result of each region's terroir.

In other words, if you were to convince a tea master to produce the same type of tea from the same cultivars but from bushes grown in southeast China, Taiwan, and Japan, you would undoubtedly taste, smell, and see a difference. It is this difference that is the true expression of each region's terroir. Unfortunately, it is very difficult,

Without access to the specialty teas of China, much of the twentieth-century world lost contact with the great teas created throughout China's complex several-thousand-year tea history. In the twentieth century, the Western tea industry also began exclusively marketing teas from countries that until relatively recently had not been tea-producing countries. Even with the world shifting its focus away from China and toward the old colonial states, the Chinese tea industry and, to a smaller extent, the Japanese industry still stand supreme in their ability to offer incredibly refined small-batch, single-estate teas of every type. In fact, Chinese and Japanese teas provide the benchmark from which all other teas are judged, making them the best suited for demonstrating not only the processing that distinguishes the myriad of teas but also the importance of terroir, land, and place in crafting a delightful tea. In other words, understanding Chinese and Japanese tea is essential to understanding tea.

EFFECT OF TERROIR

As China increasingly opened its borders and expanded trade in the 1980s, 1990s, and early twenty-first century, tea companies saw an opportunity to turn their attention away from selling the commodity teas of the twentieth century and toward selling the great specialty teas of China. The most obvious technique for doing this was to make parallels between the wine industry and the tea industry. For, just as wine developed and evolved over centuries from numerous grape varietals and technological innovations emerging from discrete villages and regions around the world, so too did China's tea production develop.

if not impossible, to find such a flight of tea. Therefore, if you seek to better understand a region's terroir and why certain regions are revered for their teas, you must simply drink a lot of tea from that region. After going through such a wonderful exercise, you will eventually understand the unique terroir of that region as you will begin to taste similarities within the different teas. These similarities are created only through the similar geological, geographical, and environmental uniqueness that they share.

CHINA'S GROWING REGIONS

In discussing tea-growing regions in China, it is easiest to divide China into four main production regions, each of which has its own unique history, style, and types of teas produced: Jiangbei, Jiangnan, southern, and southwest.

JIANGBEI (RIVER NORTH)

The Jiangbei region consists of the areas north of the Yangtze River, including the Shandong, Anhui, Henan, Shaanxi, Gansu, and the northern part of Jiangsu Provinces. Because this region has a low average temperature of around 59°F (15°C), its climate is conducive to growing sublime green teas. This low average temperature allows the tea leaves to grow slowly, which allows the teas to obtain more flavor. There are numerous famous teas from this region. Two of the most famous green teas from this region are Xin Yang Mao Jian (Henan) and Liu An Gua Pian (Anhui). It is also home to the now famous Qimen black tea (Anhui).

JIANGNAN

The Jiangnan region, which produces approximately two-thirds of all of China's tea, is located in the middle to lower regions of the Yangtze River and includes the Zhejiang, Jiangxi, Hubei, Hunan, and the southern parts of Anhui and Jiangsu Provinces. Because the average temperature in this region can be very hot, many of the tea estates are located higher in the mountains where the temperatures are cooler. With its four seasons and plentiful rain throughout the spring and summer, this area produces an incredible diversity of tea types. With that said, in 2013, the region suffered one of the worst droughts on record with some estates

If you seek a better understanding of the characteristics making each of these four regions unique, start with one region's classic teas and taste multiple iterations of that one tea. This will give you an appreciation for how the same type of tea will differ from one village to another. Similar to how sommeliers understand wine's variety by becoming acquainted with the primary wines from each region, you can acquire a better appreciation for a region's unique teas by sampling a flight of the same tea from the same region.

reporting that they lost almost three-quarters of their tea plants. Jiangnan is perhaps most famous for its green teas: Longjing/Dragonwell (Zhejiang), Bi Luo Chun (Jiangsu), and Huang Shan Mao Feng (Anhui).

LINGNAN/SOUTHERN

China's Lingnan/southern region consists of the Guangdong, Fujian, and Hainan Provinces as well as the Guangxi Zhuang Autonomous Region. The Lingnan/southern region is the birthplace of white, oolong, and black tea. This region's oolong tea is especially revered because much of the region contains thick red clay that provides a very distinctive flavor and aroma for the oolong teas produced in this region. The region is considered one of the best in the world for growing tea primarily because the growing season is very long, it receives ample rain, and it has very cool annual temperatures. While this region is the prime region for white, oolong, and black tea, it is not as well known for its green teas, which are not of a particularly high quality. It has become well known, however, for its scented green teas, especially jasmine tea (see "Green Tea" for more information). Finally, there has been resurgence in the popularity of black teas from this region in large part due to an ever-increasing popularity for the now famous Jin Jun Mei (Fujian) black tea. The region is also home to Bai Lin Congfu, Zhenghe Gongfu, and Tangyang Congfu, also known as the three famous Fujian reds. The most famous teas of this region are the oolong teas from the Fujian Province: Tie Guan Yin (Anxi), Da Hong Pao (WuYi Shan), Shui Jin Gui (WuYi Shan), Tie Luo Han (WuYi Shan), and Bai Ji Guan (WuYi Shan) as well as its famous white tea, Baihao Yinzhen (Fuding).

SOUTHWEST

The southwest region is universally considered the birthplace of tea and includes Sichuan, Yunnan, Guizhou, and part of the Tibet Autonomous Region. This region is best known for the production of Pu'erh and other dark teas, although it also produces very fine black teas. The teas produced in the southwest tend to vary greatly in taste and appearance because the region's soil has some of the highest organic content in all of China. Unlike the Jiangbei and Jiangnan regions, the southwest does not produce a famous green tea, although, as with most regions in China, the region produces interesting green teas for domestic consumption. In addition to its famous Pu'erh teas, the southwest produces sublime black teas such as Dian Hong (Yunnan).

Producing more than 45 percent of all of Japan's tea, the Shizuoka prefecture produces the most tea in Japan. In the past three years the Shizuoka prefecture has also become infamous as the first major tea-producing prefecture in which the government closed tea estates due to radioactive contamination from the Fukushima Daiichi nuclear disaster. Although the levels in the large majority of these tea plants were below any level of concern, in June 2011 France intercepted and destroyed 162 kilograms of Shizuoka green tea that was shipped to Paris after the French government detected radioactive cesium above the European Union limit. This negative publicity crippled the prefecture's industry and has caused great concern to the farmers and producers in this region.

JAPAN'S GROWING REGIONS

It is generally believed that Japan planted its first tea trees sometime in the twelfth century. As it has been for nine hundred years, Japan almost exclusively produces green teas (it does produce some interesting black teas for its domestic market, however). Of the tea produced in Japan, it is estimated that almost 90 percent of its production is used for domestic consumption. And, although most of Japan's prefectures produce tea, it is generally conceived that twelve of its forty-seven prefectures are renowned for tea production.

The twelve most famous prefectures for Japanese tea production are Aichi (Nishio in Aichi is one of the largest production areas for Matcha), Fukuoka (generally regarded as the prefecture producing some of Japan's finest quality Gyokuro, considered one of the finest Japanese green teas), Gifu, Kagoshima, Kumamoto, Kyoto (its Uji region is home to Japan's first tea plantings and is considered by many to be the emotional center of Japanese tea culture), Mie, Miyazaki, Nagasaki, Saga, Saitama, and Shizuoka.

The Japanese prefectures famous for their tea production all have their own climate, soil, and growing conditions and therefore produce their own unique teas worthy of a lifetime of exploration and discovery. Because the Japanese, like the Chinese, have had hundreds of years of experimentation, it is also a good place to discover the importance of the land's terroir in creating an excellent tea.

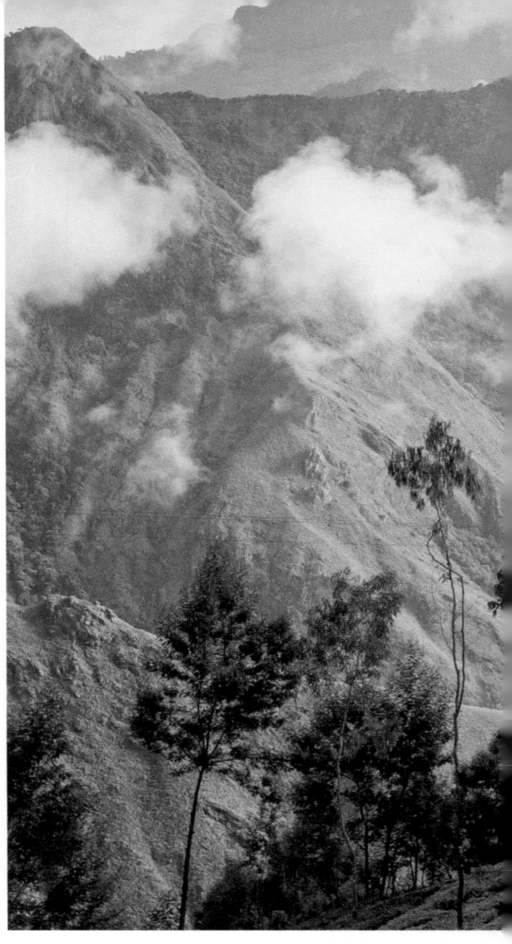

SOUTH ASIA'S GROWING REGIONS

Tea has been growing in south Asia for thousands of years, but it has only been about 150 years since the region began planting tea bushes for market. As consumers are looking to taste more varieties of tea, these teas are being recognized for their quality and uniqueness.

Over the past twenty years, India has been aggressive promoting its specialty teas. With the Indian government liberalizing its laws, growers are no longer required to sell their leaves at an Indian tea auction house. Therefore, these growers are starting to experiment with producing specialty tea, not just the higher-volume commodity teas largely associated with India's tea industry. The three primary growing areas in India are found around the Darjeeling region in the northern section of the state of West Bengal, the state of Assam, and the Nilgiri mountains in southwest India. Assam is a state in the northeast section of India—directly north of Bangladesh—and is the location in which the English first brought attention to the indigenously growing *Camellia sinensis* var. *assamica*. Today, most of the teas grown in Assam are the more bitter, astringent, full-bodied teas made from this now famous tea variety.

Over the past one-hundred years people have propagated tea plants in such diverse places as India, Nepal, Indonesia, Kenya, and even North America and have begun producing green teas with these plants. In comparison to the traditional tea regions in China and Japan, these new experiments pale in comparison to the variety, quality, and refinement of the Chinese and Japanese teas. China and Japan stand apart as the benchmark for tea lovers. It is for this reason that throughout this book I focus primarily on the Chinese and Japanese teas and discuss teas of other regions when their history or uniqueness warrants. This is not to say that there are not histories and teas worthy of attention. Rather, I simply believe that the story of tea's art and craft can best be explained primarily through the traditional Chinese and Japanese teas.

Darjeeling is a semi-autonomous district located just west of Assam and just east of Nepal in the northern portion of India's state of West Bengal. The tea estates in this district are situated amongst the Mahabarhat Mountains (also known as the Lesser Himalaya Range). Unlike the black teas made in Assam, Darjeeling black tea is made from cultivars of the *Camellia sinensis* var. *sinensis* plant, most of which the English originally transplanted from China's Fujian Province.

Nilgiri is the largest tea-growing district in southern India. Most of the tea grown in this region is grown in the Western Ghats mountain range in the states of Tamil Nadu and Kerala. Much of the tea grown in Nilgiri is very low grade and used for black tea blends. It is an important component in a lot of tea blends because tea from this region often has a very strong flavor. Recently, producers in Nilgiri have begun experimenting with producing higher-graded black teas as well as green and white tea.

SRI LANKA/CEYLON

Tea growing was introduced to Sri Lanka in the middle of the nineteenth century, but the industry did not grow until the Sri Lankan coffee crop was decimated by coffee blight in the 1860s and 1870s. The coffee blight was so bad that almost all of Sri Lanka's coffee crop was destroyed within ten years of exposure, forcing most of Sri Lanka's coffee growers to replant their coffee fields with tea. The mountains in central Sri Lanka make for ideal tea-growing conditions because they receive ample rain and cool temperatures. Most of Sri Lanka's tea production is dedicated to the production of its famous black tea: Ceylon.

NEPAL

The East India Company began planting tea in Nepal in the 1860s, at the same time that it began planting tea in Darjeeling. Nepal and Darjeeling share a similar climate and geography and largely grow tea from similar cultivars. Therefore, Nepal's black tea tastes and smells similar to Darjeeling's. Throughout the twentieth century, however, Nepal's government isolated the country from foreign trade and investment and the industry virtually collapsed. In the past twenty years, the government has made a concerted effort to revitalize its tea industry, and it is now possible to find Nepal's exotic-tasting teas in markets around the world.

TEA'S CHEMISTRY

CHEMICAL GROUPS

The main chemical groups found in tea are polyphenols, flavanols, alkaloids, amino acids, carbohydrates, minerals, and vitamins. All of these chemicals play important but different roles in the taste, aroma, appearance, and health benefits of tea. The ratio of each of these chemicals is dependent on the variety of tea leaf, the cultivar, the soil, the time of year the leaf was plucked, and the atmospheric conditions at the time of plucking.

ANTIOXIDANTS

Flavanols are found naturally in the leaves of the Camellia sinensis plant and represent one of the most marketable chemical groups in tea. Although there are many flavanols in a tea leaf, the flavanols receiving the most attention and having the most interest are the antioxidants epicatechins and catechins. Of these two flavanols, epigallocatechin gallate (EGCG) is the most abundant catechin found in tea, and it also happens to be the antioxidant with the most promise for its presumed health benefits.

It is now generally agreed that tea has approximately 8–10 percent more antioxidants than any other fruit or vegetable, that antioxidants generally protect cells from oxidative stress (damage caused by overly reactive oxygen in your body), and that oxidative stress plays a significant role in various human diseases and ailments. It is not clear, however, how various antioxidants affect different cells or whether all antioxidants affect cells in the same way—all important questions considering antioxidants come in various forms, and the antioxidants found in tea are not necessarily the same antioxidants found in other fruits and vegetables. Finally, studies have shown that antioxidants are found in great numbers in all types of tea, even though roughly 25–40 percent of EGCG is converted into theaflavins, thearubigins, and theabrownins during oxidation of oolong and black tea.

CAFFEINE

Another important chemical in tea, and perhaps the most economically significant chemical, is the alkaloid trimethylxanthine, or caffeine. Caffeine is by far the most consumed psychoactive drug in the world, with estimates suggesting that over 90 percent of all adults in the world consume caffeine every day. Tea is one of the most widely used means for consuming caffeine. For the tea plant, caffeine serves two natural purposes: It is a natural insecticide, killing pests that ingest it; and it strengthens the memory of the bugs that pollinate the tea plant, allowing them to return year after year to pollinate the plant's flowers. For humans, caffeine is best known for its effects on the central nervous system as it stimulates the central nervous system to create energy.

Caffeine is a relatively stable chemical and is not diminished nor increased during any of tea's production processes. It does decrease in the leaf, however, the longer the leaf grows on the tea plant. That is to say, caffeine levels are generally the greatest in younger, immature leaves. So, the younger a leaf is when plucked, the more caffeine it is likely to have. It is often incorrectly believed that black tea

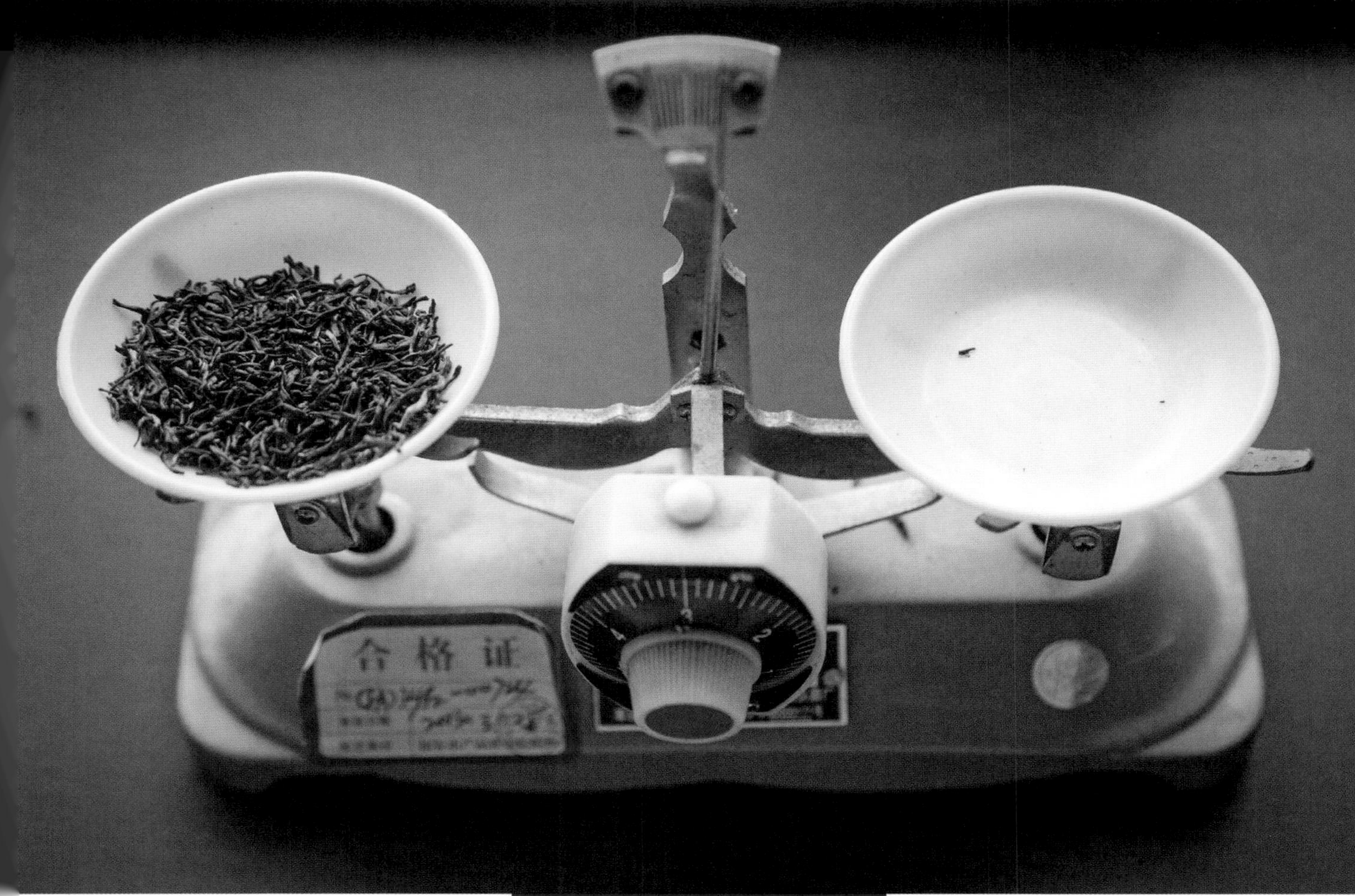

has the greatest amount of caffeine of the six types of tea. Such belief is not necessarily true, although it is easy to speculate as to why this is so.

Throughout the twentieth century, teas grown in the old colonial territories dominated the world's black tea market. The vast majority of these teas are produced from the leaves of *Camellia sinensis* var. *assamica*, leaves that generally contain more caffeine than the leaves from var. *sinensis*. Therefore, the black teas made from var. *assamica* generally do have more caffeine than black teas made from var. *sinensis*. This, however, is not to say that black tea as a type contains more caffeine than other types of teas. It simply means that people's perceptions of teas have been biased based on the market conditions created over the past one hundred years. To anticipate the caffeine of a particular tea, it is important that you know not only the age of the leaf when plucked but also from what variety the tea came.

In 2008, the *Oxford Journal of Analytical Toxicology* published a paper entitled "Caffeine Content of Brewed Teas" in which the authors found "no observable trend in caffeine concentration" due to the type of tea. The most important factors for determining a tea's caffeine level are as follows:

1. Variety of tea
2. Clonal variety
3. Organic content of soil and/or fertilizer
4. Age of leaves
5. Heat of water used for steeping
6. Steeping time
7. Quantity of leaves used

THEANINE

Another very important yet often overlooked chemical found naturally in tea is the amino acid theanine. Theanine has been found in high doses to have psychoactive effects on the brain. It also has been linked throughout history as the chemical responsible for people feeling relaxed when drinking tea and as the chemical responsible for the often-experienced "tea high." Although chemists are currently conducting tests to determine the exact effects of theanine, it is generally agreed that theanine likely creates positive mood-altering effects. Finally, theanine is known to have a very distinctive umami taste and is largely responsible for the earthy, "wet stone" taste of many teas.

CHANGES TO CHEMICAL COMPOSITION

In addition to the chemicals naturally found in tea, there are sets of other chemicals that are formed during tea's various manufacturing processes. Perhaps the most important of these chemical changes takes place during the oxidation process. Although the oxidation process is quite technical, understanding what takes places during this process goes a long way in understanding how oxidation drastically affects the taste, aroma, and qualities of tea.

OXIDATION

Tea leaves contain the polyphenol oxidase enzyme known more accurately as polyphenol oxidase or PPO. The PPO enzyme contains copper ions that react with oxygen in such a way that they transform a tea leaf's aromatic compounds known as polyphenolic compounds into organic compounds called quinones. When the cellular structure of a tea leaf is intact, the PPO enzyme's copper ions cannot react with oxygen. If the cellular structure is ruptured by physical means or heat, then the PPO enzyme becomes exposed and the tea leaf's polyphenolic compounds will begin to transform into quinones as the PPO enzyme begins to interact with the oxygen.

Once formed, these quinones react with proteins located in the tea leaf to create theaflavins, the most important of which is melanin—a black-red pigment. The more the PPO enzyme transforms polyphenolic compounds into quinones, the more melanin is created and the more a leaf turns black. Thus, lightly oxidized oolongs generally have a dark green appearance, whereas more-fully oxidized oolongs and black teas have a very dark red or coppery appearance.

The polyphenolic compounds transformed during the oxidation process are generally caffeic acid (a phenolic acid not to be confused with caffeine), epicatechin, and catechin (a natural phenol and antioxidant). The fact that epicatechins and catechins (antioxidants) are converted during oxidation is the reason there is a decrease in the amount of certain antioxidants between black tea and green tea. Unfortunately, this is also the reason why many people mistakenly believe green and white teas are more "healthy" than black or oolong teas. Although a large percentage of EGCG is transformed during the oxidation process of oolong and black teas, there still remains an extraordinarily high amount of EGCG when the oxidation process ends as well as the other antioxidants and essential vitamins and minerals naturally occurring in a tea leaf.

TASTE CHANGES

In addition to these biochemical changes, the higher temperatures used during the oxidation process degrade the tea leaf's amino acids, allowing these amino acids to interact with the leaf's carbohydrates and to produce new flavor compounds. These newly created flavor compounds are experienced as the classic "malty" aroma that is a hallmark of black tea.

PART 2:
TECHNIQUE

WATER

THE WATER UNDERSTANDS
CIVILIZATION WELL;
IT WETS MY FOOT, BUT PRETTILY,
IT CHILLS MY LIFE, BUT WITTILY,
IT IS NOT DISCONCERTED,
IT IS NOT BROKEN-HEARTED:
WELL USED, IT DECKETH JOY,
ADORNETH, DOUBLETH JOY:
ILL USED, IT WILL DESTROY,
IN PERFECT TIME AND MEASURE
WITH A FACE OF GOLDEN PLEASURE
ELEGANTLY DESTROY.

—R. W. EMERSON

WATER: TEA'S POET

Tea is but the mixing of water with leaves. However, reducing tea to such basic and primitive elements fails to capture the mystery and poetry that is the keystone to tea's history and culture. Mention the word tea and open a psychological door that transports you to rainy days, long meandering conversations, family picnics, romantic dinners, or nights with a book and a fire. Tea triggers such emotions if you come from a country imbued with a strong tea culture or if you come from the United States—a country in which the word tea is rarely found qualifying the word culture. But, how can the mixing of water and leaves unleash such strong memories and emotions? Surely there must be more to tea than a quick steeping of a leaf with warm water.

To help understand tea's effect on the subconscious and to gain greater insight into how we react to tea, it might be helpful to focus on the historical significance of water in literature, poetry, and religion. Whereas the tea leaf and its processing explains much of the symbolism related to the art and craft of tea, water is the psychological trigger from which we derive much of our emotional reactions to tea. It is for this reason that if we remind ourselves of the importance of water as a symbol in the great arts, we may obtain a better understanding of water's effect on our relationship to tea and how this relationship affects our enjoyment of tea.

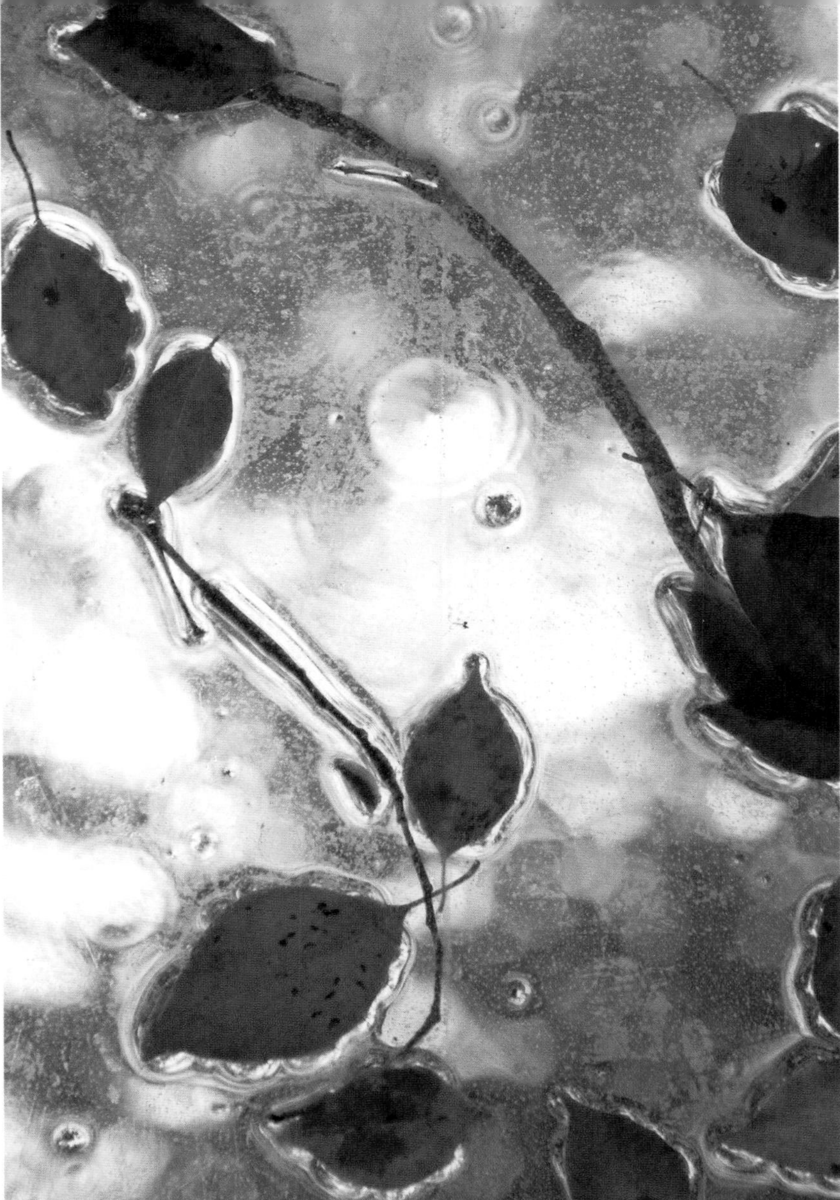

WATER AS METAPHOR

Regardless of the tradition or myth, water invariably represents the most powerful and important metaphor in that tradition or myth. In virtually all of the world's religions, water is not only a powerfully important metaphor, it is also usually synonymous with life itself.

Therefore, water indubitably plays an important metaphorical role in our worldviews and likely imports emotional content into our own subconscious.

The easiest way to demonstrate the belief that water, and hence tea, holds a privileged place in our subconscious is to quickly survey some of the world's great religions. Such an elementary survey provides a gateway into understanding the metaphorical importance of water with tea as well as our emotional reaction to tea. Or, stealing a metaphor from Greek mythology, a reflection on some of the world's religious traditions may allow us a sip from the Mnemosyne spring while avoiding taking drinks from the spring of Lethe.

WATER AS CREATOR OF THE WORLD

Not only does the term *Hindu* come from the Sanskrit term *Sindhu*, meaning river, but the Rig Veda (the earliest text in the Sanatana Dharma traditions) provides that it was water from heavenly rivers that created our universe.

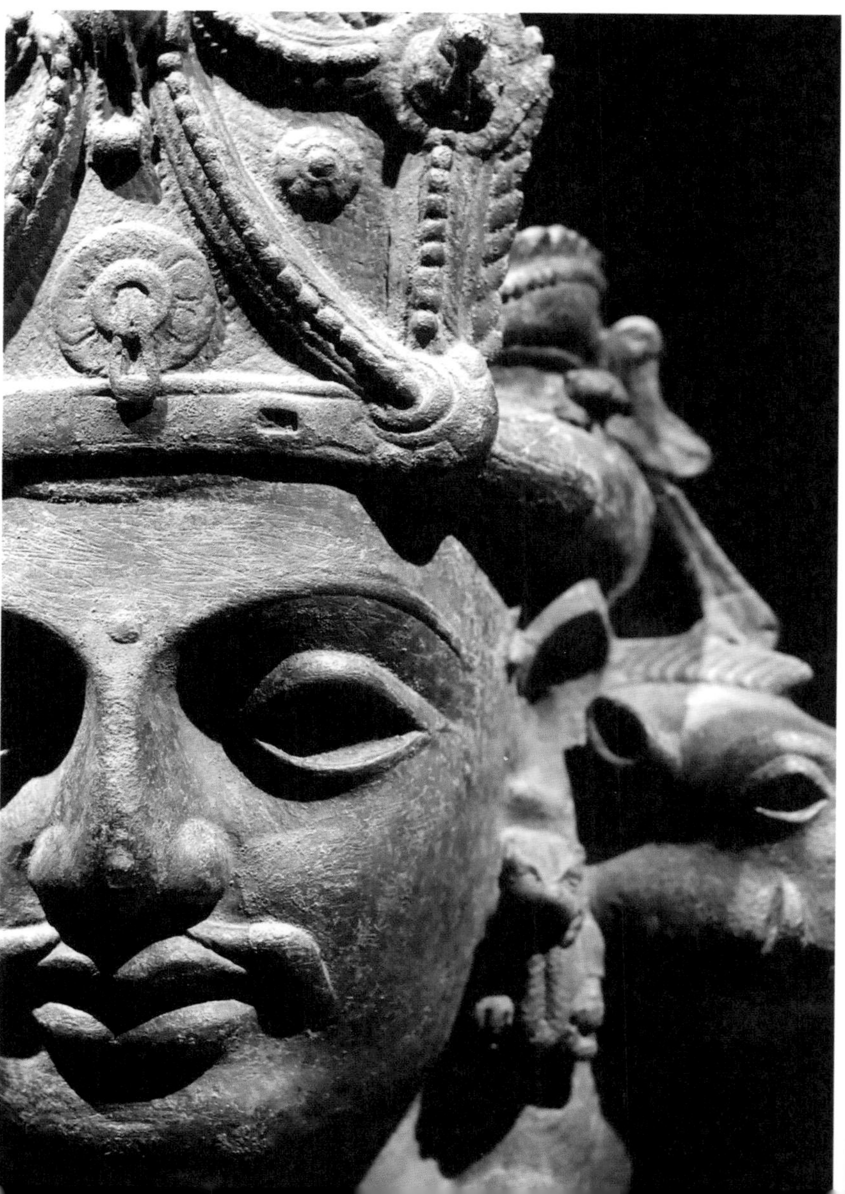

The Rig Veda teaches that prior to the creation of our world, an evil demon named Vritra blocked these heavenly rivers and trapped the water from flowing and creating the universe. Thus, Vritra kept Earth sterile, infertile, and empty. In order to release the water from heaven, the king of gods, Indra, fought and killed Vritra. Upon killing Vritra, Indra unblocked the rivers and allowed the water to flow and to create the world. Seeing water through the lens of the Rig Veda suggests that water as a symbol is potentially more important than merely a liquid that keeps us hydrated; it is the very thing that created us!

WATER AS GIFT OF LIFE

Chinese mythology provides that the world began as nothing but water controlled by the mythical dragon, a dragon from which the Chinese believe they themselves directly descend. Only after the water was transformed into vapor was the world created. In this way, water is valued not only as the cause of life but also as a gift from the creator: a gift of continued life.

WATER AS SPIRITUAL GUIDE

The Buddhists transformed the representation of water from being the direct cause of life into a metaphor of one's spiritual quest toward mindfulness. Perhaps the best example of this worldview is the Buddhists' use of a river to represent the "middle way" or path to enlightenment. This metaphor suggests that one must direct his life in a way that flows freely between decadence and deprivation, similar to how water flows between the banks of a riverbed. The Buddhists seemingly elevated water from a mere refreshing liquid into a spiritual guide.

WATER AS RIGHTEOUS LIFE

The Bible, in turn, accounts of a great flood in which God, during an age of decadence and debauchery, destroyed the earth's creatures by flooding the land with rain for forty days and forty nights. In so doing, God created a more pure world by bathing it in water. Notably, he did not use fire from within the earth; he used water from above the earth. The "water-as-purity" metaphor evolved further as the Christians began viewing water as a symbol by which one could purify one's soul. This transformation is illustrated in their tradition of the baptism, an individual's spiritual rite of passage into Christendom conducted through the introduction of water to the individual. In this way, water can be understood as not only an essential element of life but also an essential element for a righteous life!

Assuming that one or more of these traditions is imbued in our own subconscious, it seems reasonable that tea, a beverage created only through water, is capable of triggering significant psychological triggers in all of us.

WATER: TEA'S CHEMIST

Cultures around the world have certainly given water the respect that it deserves. Yet, what do these traditions have to do with making a cup of tea? A cynic might be quick to dismiss such discussions of myth and metaphor as the very thing that detracts people from drinking tea over less metaphor-laden drinks such as coffee or soda. Such cynicism might persuade us to discuss tea through scientific language instead of through poetry and metaphor.

When I use such reductionistically scientific language, however, I feel great ambivalence because I know that tea stands apart from the world's other great beverages precisely because of its tendency to be imagined through beautifully poetic and literary devices.

It is true that one can view water as a mere ingredient easily dissected into variables of temperature, chemicals, pH levels, and proper aeration. Unfortunately, focusing on such ultratechnical aspects of tea may actually destroy the poetry and beauty inherent in the sharing of a cup of tea and, thus, diminish our relationship to tea. If discussions about tea focus only on the technical aspects—such as the grades of leaves, chemical analysis, subvarieties, cultivars, terroir, and sources of water—we may lose tea to the proverbial altar of pretentiousness.

What does a discussion on the proper aeration of water mean to a chai wallah in Mumbai who was naturally taught to pour the hot masala chai from one container to another at two to four feet? On one hand, by pulling the chai he creates a more enhanced body and, thus, a better mouthfeel, making the tea actually taste better. But, on the other hand, if you try explaining mouthfeel to the chai wallah, he will probably look at you like you are drab and uninteresting. If asked, the chai wallah will invariably tell you that he goes through such ceremony because people enjoy it. It provides a moment of magic for someone's otherwise routine morning. More important than improving the taste of the tea, the chai wallah focuses on creating an experience, a moment that elevates a simple morning tea into something greater than merely a caffeine and sugar rush.

In this way, it is prudent to appreciate, to respect, and to be cognizant of the mysticism and magic associated with tea and its culture whenever we begin technically analyzing tea.

ANALYZING WATER

Tea's tastes and smells are very subtle. Therefore, it is important that you brew your tea with high-quality water that does not impart its own taste or smell. Choosing the right water with which to brew your tea should be no more complicated than choosing a clear, odorless, uncontaminated, and refreshing water.

When chemists test for water quality, they generally test for the presence of thirteen different substances: alkalinity, color, pH, taste, odor, dissolved metals and salts, presence of microorganisms, dissolved metals and metalloids, dissolved organics, radon, heavy metals, pharmaceuticals, and hormone analogs. Needless to say, one could work oneself into a dark hole figuring out the perfect pH for each of his favorite teas or spend weeks joining online debates on the absolute maximum dissolved metals and salts one should allow in his tea water.

To maintain the poetic beauty inherent in the sharing of a cup of tea, tea preparation should approximate an art more than a science and you should be vigilant in focusing on the enjoyment and camaraderie that comes from sharing tea rather than on perfecting the minutiae for making the "perfect" cup of tea. This is not to say that water is not important. It is! In fact, in some ways water is as important as tea leaves for making a delicious cup of tea. With that in mind, I recommend considering a few commonsense issues when choosing what source of water to use in brewing your tea so that you can maximize not only the enjoyment of your tea but also the taste of your tea.

CLARITY

Without question, water used for making tea must be clear. One of the primary ways of evaluating and enjoying a cup of tea is simply by looking at it. If you start with cloudy water, you will end up with cloudy tea, and cloudy tea is often a difficult tea to enjoy. Furthermore, our minds actually begin "tasting" food and drinks well before we put the food or drink in our mouths. In a classic experiment, psychologists in France provided a panel of wine tasters a series of white wine and asked for the wine tasters to evaluate the wines. Unbeknownst to the wine tasters, the psychologists made the white wine appear red by adding an odorless food coloring. When evaluating the wines, the wine tasters all used descriptors commonly used for red wine. Not one taster used descriptors associated with white wines. The results of this experiment reconfirmed how our sight fundamentally alters the way we experience and taste food and drink. If you want to have an outstanding experience with your teas, start with clear water and make clear tea!

ODOR

In "Sensing Tea" (page 92), I outline the olfactory referral illusion, how we routinely mistake retronasal olfaction for "taste," and how this mistake allows us to talk about a tea's "floral" or "earthy" taste. Most important in that discussion is the fact that smell is vitally important to how we taste or experience tea. In fact, in most cases our smell actually dictates what we taste. With this in mind, the importance of using odorless water for making tea cannot be overstated.

AERATION (CRISPNESS)

Most water contains molecules of dissolved oxygen. People often refer to water containing high levels of dissolved oxygen as tasting "crisp," whereas they refer to water containing low levels of dissolved oxygen as tasting "dull." A crisp-tasting tea is unequivocally preferable to a dull-tasting tea. Therefore, it is important that your water be aerated; it should contain dissolved oxygen.

Although you can easily get caught up with analyzing dissolved oxygen's effect on the taste of your tea, I am content with a couple of rules of thumb that I believe represent commonsense practices you probably already discovered on your own, even if you are not cognizant of your discoveries.

Bottled water often contains very little dissolved oxygen and often tastes dull. Therefore, most bottled water is not a preferred source of water for making tea. The dull taste associated with bottled water could have many causes. It may have been distilled (distillation strips most of the dissolved oxygen from the water as well as the water's mineral content), it may have sat for a long time, or it may have lacked dissolved oxygen at the source. Regardless, if your only source of clear, odorless, uncontaminated water is from a bottle, then you should find a bottled water that tastes the most crisp and then relax and enjoy your tea.

The process of heating, cooling, and then reheating water evaporates water's dissolved oxygen. I find it common throughout the world for people to keep a pot of water on the stove—teakettles! When it comes time to make tea, this stagnant water is simply reheated. Although convenient, this process of heating, cooling, and then reheating is unfortunately extremely efficient at evaporating oxygen from water. A good rule of thumb is to heat water only once. Never reheat or reboil previously heated water (or water that has been sitting out for a long period of time). Your reheated water will surely taste dull.

One of the best sources for aerated water is a naturally flowing spring. I suspect most do not have access to a naturally flowing spring, but you are in luck because kitchen faucets are also a great source for aerated water.

MINERAL CONTENT

In addition to dissolved oxygen, the concentration of dissolved solids can also affect water's taste. Although there are many soluble solids in water that could be considered when evaluating water, perhaps the most common negative issue for water is that it contains a high quantity of calcium and magnesium sulfate, also known as hard water. Water with high concentrations of calcium and magnesium sulfates has an unpleasant soda-powder taste, whereas water lacking such minerals lacks a depth of taste; like water lacking in dissolved oxygen, hard water tastes dull. The best example for this is distilled water. In contrast to hard water, distilled water is water in which most, if not all, of the water's mineral content has been removed, creating a water that tastes "flat" or "dull." As with all great things, the best water for making tea is water that contains not too much nor too little mineral content.

Further, if you ever had the displeasure of showering with hard water, you probably noticed that your soap did not lather. In fact, you probably noticed that the soap formed a precipitate (a scum) that was difficult to rinse. This effect also occurs when making tea with hard water. In addition to creating an off-taste, hard water forms a precipitate around the ring of the cup (commonly referred to as tea scum), which is unsettling, especially if you are trying to impress your guests!

Finally, confusing the issue of hard water is the fact that the term hard water is often incorrectly used to describe water with a high concentration of dissolved iron. Regardless of classification, water with a high iron concentration tastes extremely metallic and usually discolors the water. Needless to say, discolored water that tastes metallic should not be used for making tea.

Calcium and magnesium sulfates are noncarbonate compounds that do not evaporate at boil. Water containing high quantities of these compounds is referred to as "permanently hard water." Permanently hard water is different than temporary hardness, which is the term used to describe water with high quantities of calcium or magnesium carbonate compounds that evaporate at boil and are, therefore, not as big of a concern for making tea because you can simply boil off these carbonate compounds, if needed.

PREPARING TO MAKE THE PERFECT CUP OF TEA

Knowing about tea plants, cultivars, tea types, and water is interesting, but it does not get one any closer to tea's real beauty—the actual experience of drinking a delicious cup of tea. The following are considerations to help you maximize your enjoyment of tea.

CHOOSING A TEA

By adding water to the leaves of the Camellia sinensis plant, one can create a true elixir of life. Deciding what type of tea to use can be as mundane as deciding to use the ubiquitous yet dusty commodity tea in your cabinet or as memorable as deciding to use a handcrafted tea from one of the world's famous growers and producers. But, how should one decide?

Choosing a tea should never be stressful. Unfortunately, the marketing strategy for most tea companies is to overwhelm the market with choice, creating a real-life example of the famous psychological dilemma known as the paradox of choice. The paradox of choice is the title given to the two phenomena that occur when people have too great a choice. First, a person is less likely to feel happy about the choice he does choose and regrets or refuses to enjoy that which he bought (often referred to as buyer's remorse). Second, he becomes less likely to make a choice at all, essentially becoming paralyzed (often referred to as the paradox of choice).

Assuming the paradox of choice is accurate, it is unfathomable how someone new to tea should choose a tea. First, he must determine if he wants a green, white, yellow, oolong, black, or dark tea. Then he must choose what type of tea he wants. Does he want a Chinese green tea? A Japanese green tea? How about a New World green tea? God help him if he wants to try a Chinese green tea. Not only does he need to navigate the Chinese names, but he also needs to choose one among hundreds of various green teas. Good luck!

Compounding the problem is the fact that most of the teas for sale in supermarkets, and even most tea shops, are not even tea. They are tisanes, herbs, aromatics, or low-grade tea with added flavorings.

With all of this in mind, here are a few quick and easy rules that one can follow in deciding which tea to try:

The paradox of choice is best exemplified in the now famous but increasingly challenged experiment performed by psychologists Mark Lepper and Sheena Iyengar. Psychologist Barry Schwartz in his 2004 book *The Paradox of Choice* writes: "When researchers set up [in a gourmet food store] a display featuring a line of exotic, high-quality jams, customers who came by could taste samples, and they were given a coupon for a dollar off if they bought a jar. In one condition of the study, 6 varieties of the jam were available for tasting. In another, 24 varieties were available. In either case, the entire set of 24 varieties was available for purchase. The large array of jams attracted more people to the table than the small array, though in both cases people tasted about the same number of jams on average. When it came to buying, however, a huge difference became evident. Thirty percent of the people exposed to the small array of jams actually bought a jar; only 3 percent of those exposed to the large array of jams did so."

TEA IS AN AGRICULTURAL PRODUCT

Always remember that tea is an agricultural product. Like all agricultural products, there are certain seasons more suitable than others for drinking various teas. Green, white, and yellow teas all have very short shelf lives. Under even ideal circumstances these teas should be consumed within three to four months of processing. Because most classic teas are harvested and produced in early spring, these types of teas are ideal for spring and summer consumption. In other words, if you seek to experience a delicious green tea, you best not search for such a tea in February!

SEASONALITY OF TEA

Tea production is dependent on the growing conditions of each year (tea leaves cannot be plucked until the weather is suitable and the plants exhibit vigorous growth) and each tea-growing region has different seasons in which it harvests tea leaves.

MARCH

March is the month in which tea production usually begins. Tea producers in India and Nepal begin plucking leaves for black teas in early March (first flush), and producers in China begin plucking for a few of its premium teas.

APRIL

April is the busiest month for tea production, and China divides the month into multiple periods based on the lunar calendar and the spring rains. Many of China's premium teas are graded on whether the leaves were plucked before, during, or after these events. The end of April and beginning of May is also the beginning of the harvest cycle for most of Taiwan, Japan, and Korea.

MAY

At the end of spring, usually in May, tea producers in east Asia turn their attention from producing green and white teas toward the production of black tea. Late spring is also when producers begin using lower-grade tea stock to produce scented teas.

EARLY SUMMER, FALL, AND WINTER

In early summer, the tea production switches from premium black teas and scented teas to the production of oolongs and lower-grade black tea. In southeast China and Taiwan, tea producers begin production of various oolong teas. Finally, in midwinter regions in Sri Lanka begin production of Ceylon black tea, and areas of southwest China begin plucking for the production of various green and black teas.

The production of Sri Lanka's Ceylon black tea is different than the rest of the tea-producing countries because it is dependent on the monsoon rains. Further complicating this cycle is the fact that not all of the island gets the monsoon rain at the same time. Generally speaking, Ceylon production begins after the monsoon rains, sometime in July or August, and goes through the fall months (although there are regions that do not harvest tea until the winter months).

TEA'S WARMTH AND COOLNESS

Chinese speak of tea as having "warming" or "cooling" properties. That is to say, they view tea as either warming or cooling your internal organs. Under this paradigm, cooling teas such as green, yellow, and white teas are best consumed during the hot months, whereas warming teas such as black, oolong, and dark teas are best consumed during the cold months. This ideology is really no different than how Westerners view certain foods. For instance, it is a common belief that a cucumber or watermelon feels cool and always tastes best on a hot summer day, whereas beef stew tastes more delicious in the winter and actually makes you feel warmer. Similarly, it is believed that green tea makes you feel cooler in the summer months, whereas an oolong will keep you warm in the winter months. If you seek to taste a classic Chinese or Japanese tea, pick a tea that is suitable for that season and enjoy.

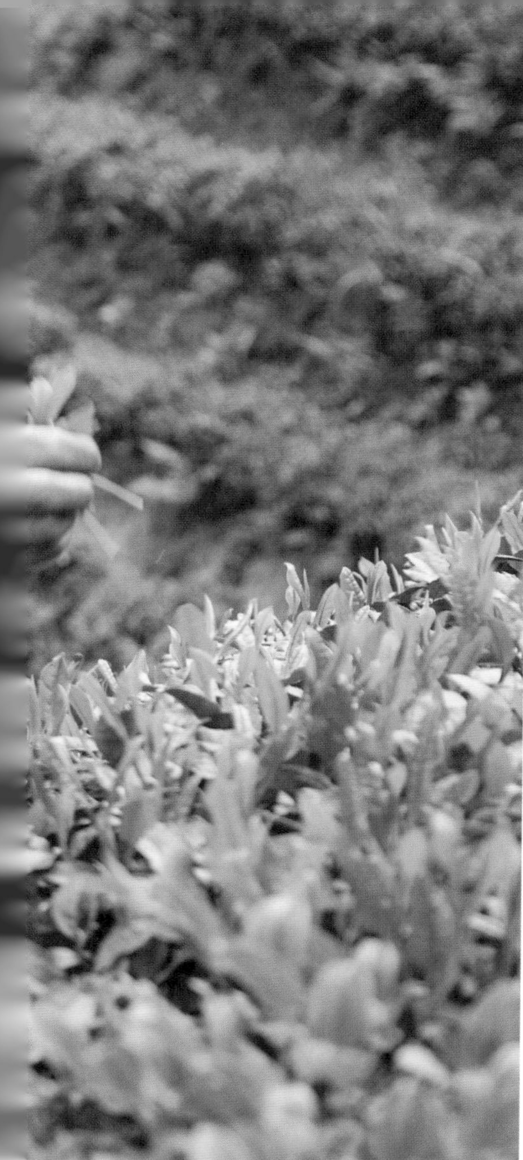

CAPITAL "T" TEA

If your goal is to understand tea, you should drink tea. Often people are introduced to tea via one of many herbal blends, aromatics, tisanes, or other crazy concoctions unfortunately labeled as "tea." If you seek to gain a better understanding of the thing that helped Buddhism spread, compelled the British empire to expand, and became the bedrock for most of the Asian cultures, then you should drink only tea. When visiting a tea shop or shopping in a grocery store, you will know that it is a tea when the ingredients list includes only one word: tea. If there are other words listed under "ingredients," find something else to purchase.

RELAX!

Part of the fun of learning about tea is not the destination but the journey. Invariably you will find teas that you do not like or do not understand. Finding such a tea does not mean that you will not like tea. It simply means that you do not like that tea. Further, most tea drinkers find that the more they drink tea, the more they revisit teas they once did not like only to find themselves enjoying them the second time. Your palate will surely change the more you drink tea and the older you become. Do not feel concerned if you hear that a tea is "famous" and you simply do not like it. All teas are not meant for everyone. Find a tea that you do enjoy, relax, and enjoy it!

SHARE

Finally, share your tea with someone you care about, be it a friend, family member, business associate, or just an acquaintance. Tea will always taste best when it is shared with someone else.

CHOOSING THE RIGHT VESSEL

To choose the right vessel in which to steep your tea, you must consider four things: material, size, shape, and quality.

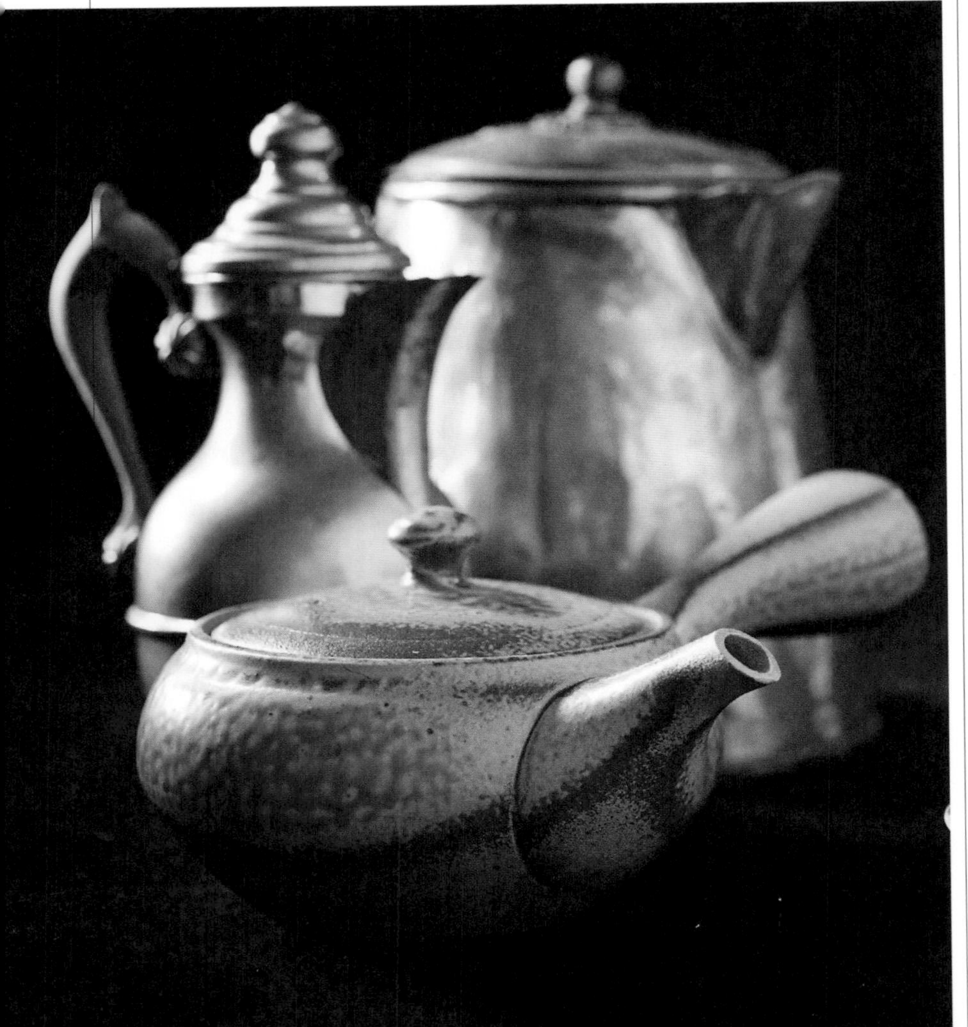

MATERIAL

Teapots are made from many different materials, but the most prominent are clay (glazed and unglazed), metal, enameled cast iron, and glass. Each material has its own advantages and disadvantages for steeping tea. The type of tea you seek to steep largely determines the type of teapot you use.

Glazed clay teapots

Glazed clay teapots are usually made from porcelain, and are therefore very thin and delicate. The thin walls and taste neutrality of the porcelain makes it ideal for delicate teas with subtle aromas and flavors.

Metal teapots

It is difficult to lump all metal teapots into one category because they come in a large variety of shapes and styles. With that said, metal teapots are primarily used in North Africa and throughout the Middle East to make very strong tea concentrates infused with fresh herbs and spices. Although metal teapots are attractive and well suited for teas with enormous flavor such as Moroccan mint tea, they are ill suited for a delicate tea such as the specialty teas from Japan and China.

Enameled cast iron teapots
Enameled cast iron teapots were originally used in China to heat water. Today, they have again become in vogue and are starting to appear as vessels in which to steep tea. With today's enamels protecting the tea from acquiring the metallic taste of the cast iron, enameled cast iron teapots are generally suitable for any type of tea. The downside of cast iron pots, however, is that it is difficult to find one small enough in size to make a complex tea.

Glass teapots
Finally, glass can be a preferable material for steeping delicate teas, especially some green, white, and yellow teas. It not only allows you to see the clarity and color of the tea, but it also allows you to enjoy the dancing leaves as they unfold during steeping. The disadvantage of glass is that it does not retain heat and therefore is not a suitable material for oolong, black, and dark tea.

SIZE

With the English and Dutch tea culture primarily driving the Western world's preferences for tea preparation, it is common to see very large teapots being used to steep tea. On one hand, these large teapots are convenient because they allow for the steeping of a higher volume of tea. As a general rule, however, the smaller the teapot, the better the tea will taste. A smaller teapot provides more control over temperature and steeping time and allows you the ability to resteep the leaves, which is the only way to experience the changes and evolution of a tea over a course of many steepings.

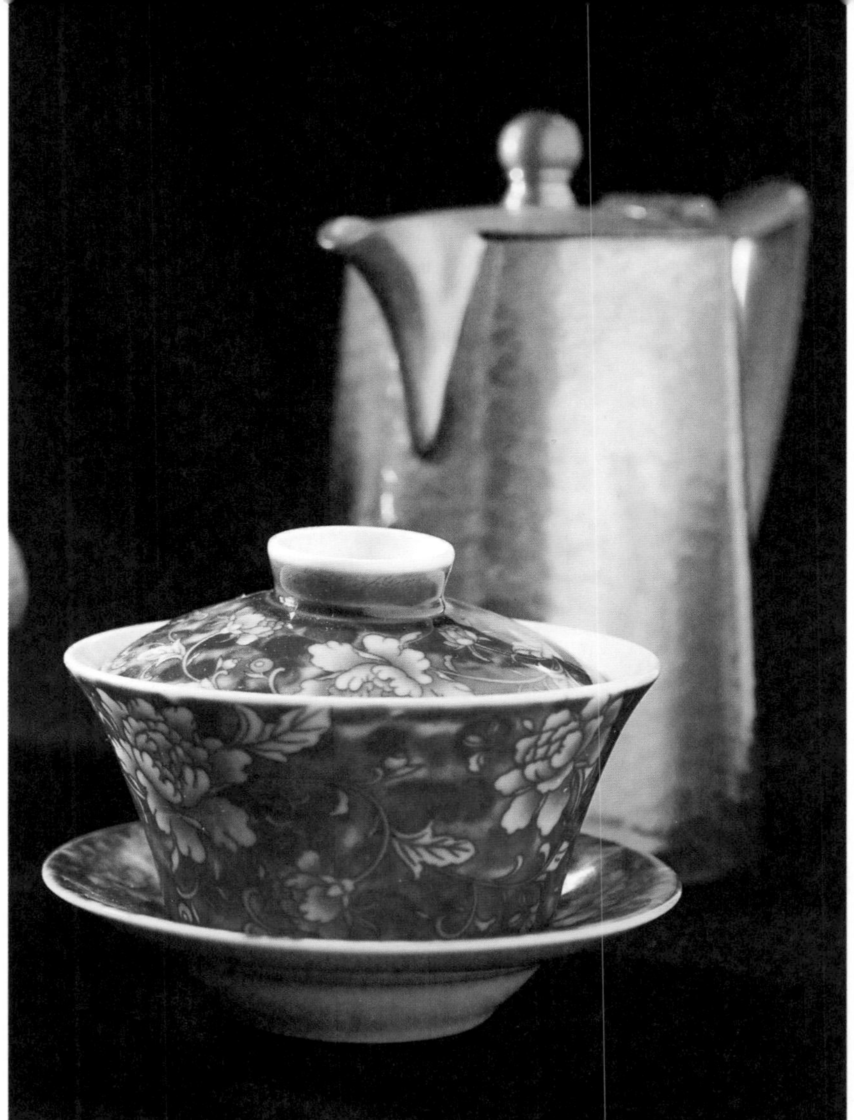

SHAPE AND QUALITY

The shape of the teapot is important because it dictates your comfort while preparing tea. So, you should not use a teapot that is too big or heavy for your hands, and you should not use a teapot that makes it difficult to easily pour your tea.

Finally, the quality of a teapot directly influences the quality of your steeped tea. Higher-quality teapots will generally last longer and will provide more predictable and uniform results from one steeping to the next.

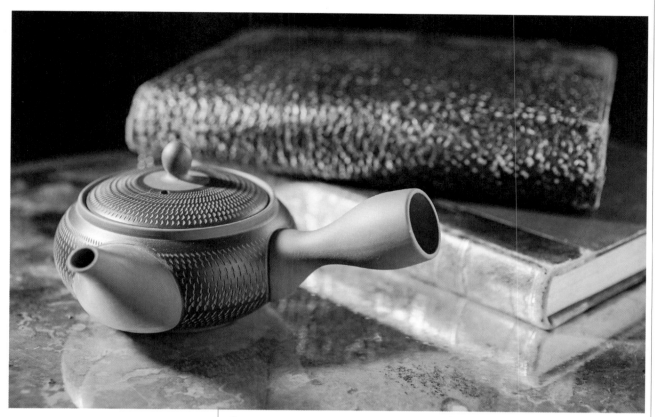

SPECIFIC TYPES OF TEAPOTS

GAIWAN

Perhaps the greatest vessel for brewing tea is one of the most simple in construction and design: the gaiwan. In use since at least the Ming dynasty (1368–1644), the gaiwan is ubiquitous in Chinese tea culture and consists of only a saucer, a bowl, and a lid. With its lid the gaiwan can be used either to decant the tea or to block the leaves while drinking directly from the gaiwan. Because of the lid's proximity to the steeping tea, the underside of the lid is also a favored way of smelling the tea's aroma.

Usually constructed from glazed porcelain, the gaiwan is considered taste and aroma neutral. That is, it does not impart any additional flavors or aromas into the tea, making it an excellent way to compare various teas. Further, a gaiwan made from porcelain is fairly efficient at retaining heat. Because of these attributes, gaiwans are used with great success for all types of tea, although some serious drinkers of black and dark teas find that gaiwans do not retain enough heat and are, therefore, not the prime vessel for steeping these types of teas.

KYUSU

The kyusu is a Japanese-designed teapot notable for its lateral handle. Instead of the Western-style teapot, which uses a design in which the spout and handle are aligned, the kyusu's handle stands at a 90-degree angle from the spout. The alignment between the handle and spout makes the pouring of the steeped tea easier and more elegant. A kyusu pot will usually have an integrated strainer inside the pot to keep the steeped leaves from blocking the flow of tea. Many of the fine Japanese kyusus created today are made from a clay with a high sandstone count. It is believed that this sandstone enhances the taste of a green tea, making the kyusu a wonderful vessel for preparing green, white, and yellow tea. Kyusu is the vessel of choice for the Senchado brewing method discussed on page 103.

↑
YIXING
Yixing pots are stoneware teapots originating from Yixing County in China's Jiangsu Province. These pots are best suited for steeping black, oolong, and dark tea. Made from the very famous clay surrounding Yixing County, Yixing pots are traditionally unglazed. This porousness benefits the flavor and aroma of a tea because over time the tannins from the tea create a coating on the inside of the pot. After multiple steepings, the Yixing pot is thought to enhance the flavor and smell of the tea because the tannin residue begins to impart a unique aroma and taste into the tea. Because of the interplay between the tannin coating and the tea, individual Yixing pots should be used only for the same type of tea. That is to say, if you use a Yixing pot to steep a black tea, you should forever after use that Yixing pot to steep only black teas.

Most Yixing pots are now mass-manufactured, making it difficult to find an authentic pot from Yixing. Traditionally, there are three criteria for classifying a Yixing pot as "well-crafted." First, the tip of the spout and the top of the handle should be level with the rim of the teapot. Second, the lid of the pot should fit snugly and be unable to move from side to side. Third, the handle and the spout should be aligned. Although most of the famous kilns in Yixing have shut down, these three variables should give you something to look for in choosing between the Yixing pots currently on the market. But, because most of today's Yixing pots are mass-produced, these variables are largely irrelevant—all the pots will be perfectly aligned. In fact, with the market consisting almost exclusively of mass-produced Yixing pots, it is now easiest to look for a pot that has slight deviations because that is a telltale sign that the pot was made by hand.

Before there were gaiwans, kyusus, or teapots, the world drank its tea from a bowl known as a chawan. Unlike teapots, a chawan was used not only to drink the tea but also to prepare the tea. Today, the chawan is used primarily in Japan for the preparation of Matcha.

CONTEMPORARY VESSELS

As stated previously, glass is often used to appreciate a tea's leaves, especially for very beautiful teas such as Silver Needle white tea. Glass, however, is not an ideal material for teas requiring longer steeping times because glass does not retain heat well. With that said, the Chinese have grown accustomed to drinking their daily green tea in a thick glass cylinder in which they simply throw a handful of dry leaves in the bottom and fill with warm water. They drink this tea throughout the day. When the liquid falls below one-third of the container, they refill it with hot water. They continue this constant steeping all day, treating their tea similar to how many people in the West use reusable containers to drink water all day.

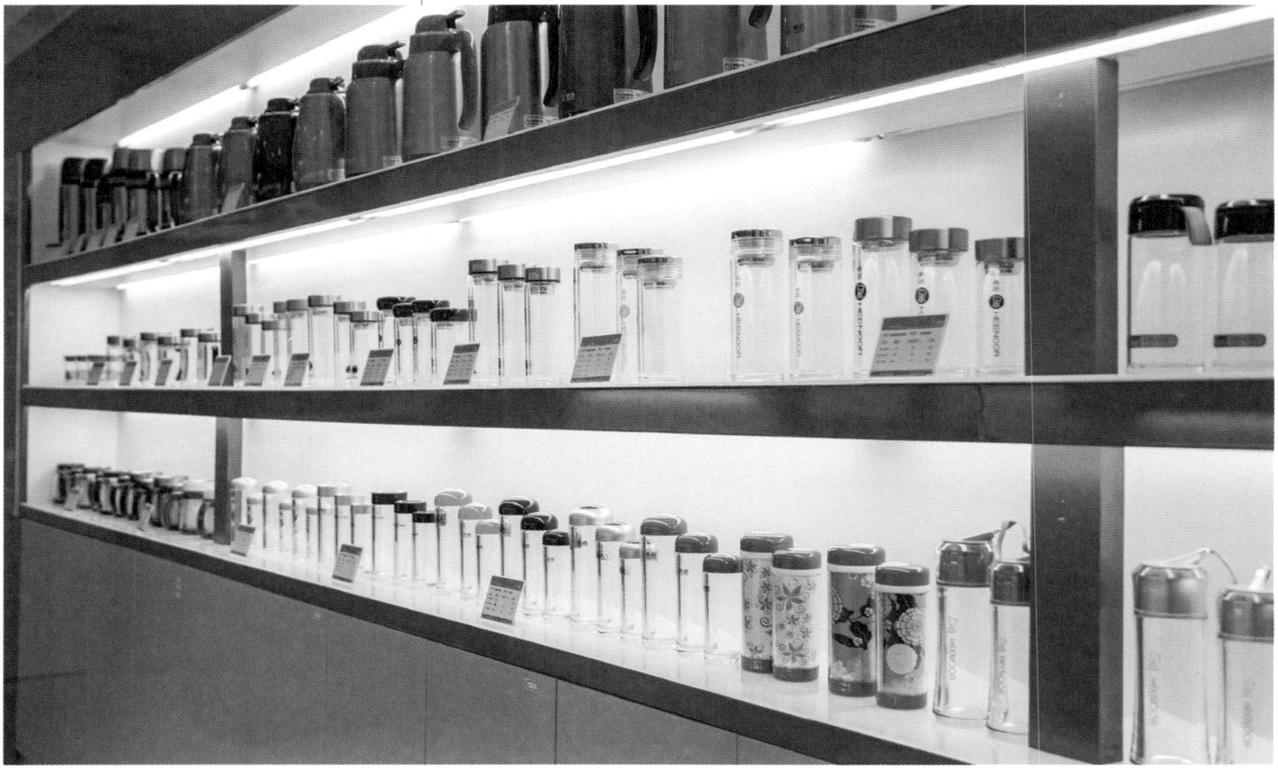

UTENSILS

Exploring, experimenting, and collecting the various styles of steeping vessels is an immensely enjoyable part of drinking tea. As such, virtually all tea shops feature a wall of steeping vessels for you to purchase. Lost in this universal marketing strategy are the various accoutrements available to make your tea preparation easier and more enjoyable as well as connect you to hundreds of years of tea culture. Following is a quick survey of various utensils that you might enjoy using for your tea preparation.

TEA TRAY

One of the most convenient accessories you should consider is the tea tray. Not to be confused with an English tea tray, which is a tray used to serve tea, the Chinese tea tray, or *cha pan*, is an essential accessory for the formal preparation of tea. Usually made from wood or stone, the tea tray is a hollow box designed to collect excess tea and water. This hollow box allows you to prepare tea without worrying about spilling, and it allows you to freely pour water on your vessels. If a tea tray seems too formal, a low-walled bowl and a nice towel are also fashionable ways for showcasing your tea preparation. (If you use your tea tray to prepare tea in the Gong Fu style, then you should also consider using tea tongs, known as *cha jia*, to clean and present the teacups.)

TEA PLATE

Known in China as a *cha he*, the tea plate is a formal way of presenting dry tea leaves. Using a tea plate allows you to measure and prepare your leaves away from the designated preparation area. It also protects the leaves remaining in the original package from coming into contact with steam and water. Finally, having the leaves premeasured into a tea plate is an easy way to showcase and evaluate the tea to be served.

INDIAN TEA STRAINER

If you are keen on making your own freshly blended teas, you should consider purchasing an Indian-style tea strainer. These strainers are designed to fit a single Western-style tea cup (8-ounce [235 ml] mug with a handle) so that you can filter the blended tea directly from the pot into your teacups. A cocktail strainer works perfectly for this as well.

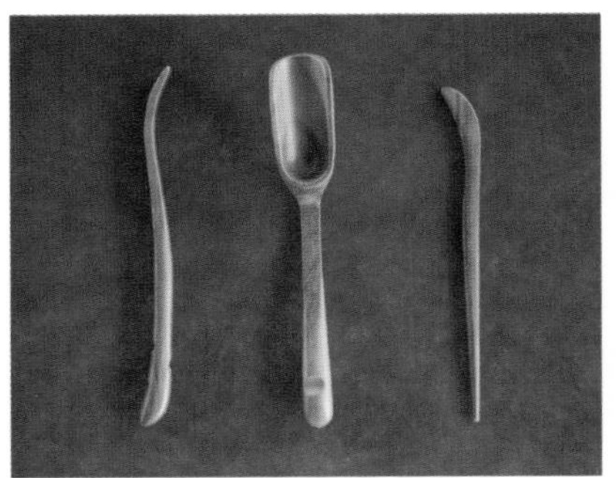

MEASURING SPOON

There are many ways to transfer leaves from their original package into a tea plate or a steeping vessel. Perhaps the easiest way is via a *cha ze*, a spatula designed just for such an activity. Simple in design, the *cha ze* helps you delicately retrieve the dry leaves and filter those leaves into the desired vessel. Other means of transferring tea are certainly possible but are usually wrought with potential pitfalls. For instance, a kitchen spoon is often too wide to retrieve gently or to accurately pour your tea leaves. Pouring the dry leaves directly from their package potentially exposes the remaining leaves to steam and humidity. And, using your fingers can introduce unwanted oils and humidity into the tea package.

POURING VESSEL AND FILTER

It is important to pour the steeped tea from the tea pot into another vessel so that the liquor is homogenous. The English sometimes do this by preparing their tea in a teakettle and then pouring the steeped tea into a teapot. The Chinese often filter their tea into a *cha hai* (a small teapot). Pouring tea into a secondary vessel not only creates a homogenous mixture, it also provides an opportunity for you to filter the liquor and to remove any unwanted leaves or sediment. This is important especially when steeping high-grade teas with a lot of pekoe dust.

TEA PETS

The Chinese have a tradition dating back to at least the 1200s in which they place clay figurines (usually in the shape of an animal) on their tea trays. These figurines, called *cha chong* or tea pets, are equal parts superstition, fun, and art. Believed to be a reflection of a person's inner soul, the selection of a tea pet is most often based on the animal's mythological powers because it is hoped that those powers transfer to the tea drinker. Having tea pets and taking care of them (pouring tea on them to keep them fed) is a delightful tradition and when done with some regularity becomes an important part of your tea enjoyment. Although often kitschy in appearance, tea pets that originate from very famous pottery regions such as Yixing that are made by experts are certainly worthy of collection.

STORING TEA

The shelf life of tea is fairly short. Green, white, and yellow tea have a shelf life of no longer than three to four months—in the best circumstances. Oolong and black teas' shelf lives are much longer with some well-constructed black teas able to maintain their quality after being stored for more than three years. Dark teas will generally store for as long as you need, so long as they are not exposed to very hot temperatures and extreme moisture.

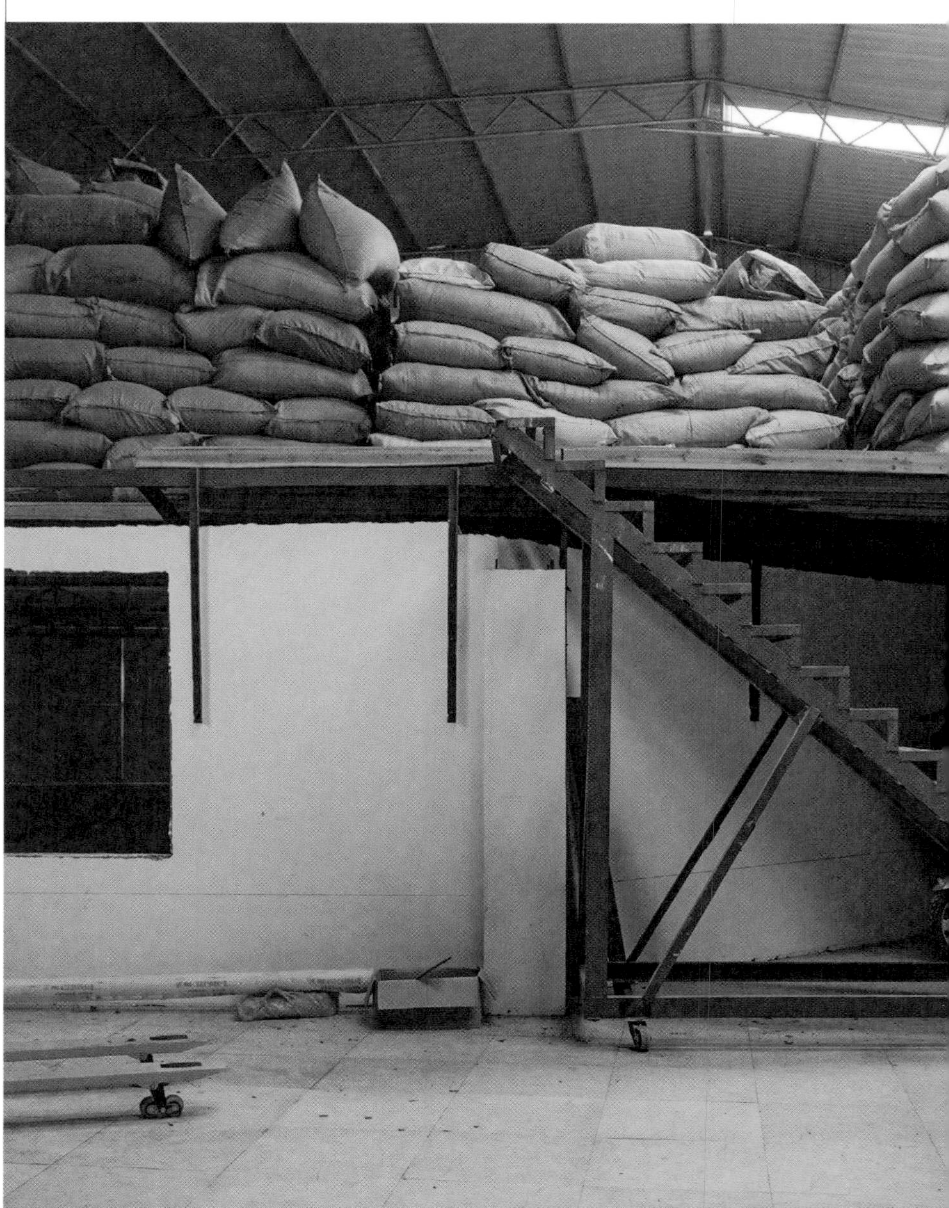

To maximize the duration of tea's taste and aroma, there are five variables you should avoid in storing your tea: sunlight, heat, moisture/humidity, odors, and air. Exposure to any of these pollutants will quickly degrade the quality of your tea and diminish its taste and aroma.

Teas are like sponges and will take on the smell and taste of any odor with which they come in contact. Some of the worst places to store your tea are refrigerators, spice drawers, pantries that contain food products with strong smells, and containers that have a heavy paint or lacquer smell. The best way to protect your tea from these contaminants is to store your tea in an opaque, airtight container in a place that is cool, dark, dry, and free of odor.

If you store all your tea in one place, be sure that each tea is stored in its own airtight container. Otherwise, the teas will begin to pick up each other's aromas, making them all taste flat. If you live in an area with high humidity, you may consider purchasing some desiccants, such as silica packets, to store directly with each of your teas. These desiccants will help keep your teas dry even in very humid conditions.

There are a multitude of containers on the market that can be used to store tea, containers both designed specifically for tea storage or just for general storage. As stated above, the best material for storing tea is material that does not attract, absorb, or give off aromas.

GLASS

Glass is usually shunned as an unsuitable storage container. Because it is so inexpensive and often comes with airtight seals, however, it can be an effective way to store tea. To use glass, you must store the container in a cabinet, desk, trunk, or other storage area that keeps the tea out of sunlight. If you have a dark place to store your glass storage containers, then glass containers such as those used for canning can be a very inexpensive and effective way to store your tea.

PLASTIC

Plastic is ubiquitous and inexpensive. Unlike glass, however, plastic often produces gases that could potentially degrade your tea. Admittedly, plastic is an easy solution for storing tea. Unfortunately, it is not a good solution.

CERAMIC

Traditional tea caddies were made from wood or ceramics. Although a collection of ceramic tea caddies can be a beautiful way to showcase your tea collection, it is difficult to find a ceramic tea caddie that is airtight.

VACUUM-SEALED TEA CADDIES

Increasingly, you can find vacuum-sealed tea caddies that actually pump out the oxygen from the container and seal the tea leaves after every use. Needless to say, such vacuum-sealing tea caddies are optimal for storing tea but also very expensive.

USING SMALLER QUANTITIES OF TEA

Finally, one of the best ways to maintain the quality of your tea is to buy only as much as you can consume in a relatively short period of time. As the tea industry switched to selling exclusively commodity teas in the twentieth century, the only consideration consumers used in choosing tea was price. So, tea companies began offering large volumes of tea for very low prices. Today, even the specialty tea market's lowest volume of tea is usually 100 grams—approximately fifty to seventy servings! That is a lot of tea to drink and to have to store, especially if you have more than one tea that you enjoy drinking. If you want to maintain the quality of your tea, consider purchasing tea in smaller volumes so as not to have to worry about long-term storage solutions.

Dark tea can improve with age, but only if it is stored properly—away from sunlight, heat, extreme moisture, and odors. Unlike other types of tea, however, dark tea should be allowed exposure to air. For this reason, most dark tea is packaged in light paper that allows the leaves to stay exposed to the ambient air. If possible, keep your dark tea stored in this paper wrapper.

EVALUATING TEA LEAVES

The most obvious ways to evaluate the quality of tea is through tasting and smelling the tea's liquor. Also important, however, is being able to evaluate the dry leaves before water is added.

KNOW YOUR TEA

Much of this evaluation is dependent on knowing what shape a particular tea should have. For instance, to evaluate a Taiwanese Bi Luo Chun you need to know that Bi Luo Chun is usually tightly rolled into a spiral, like a snail's shell. If the rolling or spiral shape is not tight, then you know the quality is not great. This knowledge only comes through experimentation and trying many variations of the same type of tea.

INSPECT FOR NON-LEAF MATERIAL

Another way to evaluate tea before steeping the leaves is to look for any sticks and twigs intermingled with the tea leaves. Tea processors can increase their profit by increasing the volume of tea they sell. The most rational way to increase the volume they sell is to sell more tea. But, tea producers can also increase profit by including sticks and twigs with their tea, an addition most people would never recognize unless they are specifically looking for it. Sticks and twigs do not necessarily alter the taste of a tea other than diluting the taste and aroma, but they drastically increase the volume of tea. Therefore, if you find sticks and twigs, it might be an indication that the tea is not of a particularly high quality.

EVALUATE LEAF CONSISTENCY

Similarly, tea can often be evaluated by discovering whether the leaves are intact (i.e., not broken) and uniform. The highest graded teas always contain fully intact, unblemished, and uniform leaves. They are not ripped or broken, and mostly do not contain markings from insects or bugs, such as holes or discoloration. In looking at the dry leaves of your tea, you should inspect the leaves for uniformity and breakage. Many teas are broken during transport; it is an unfortunate consequence of shipping teas around the world. But, if the tea contains a lot of breakage and the leaves are not uniformly shaped or sized, then this is a sign that the quality of the tea is not high.

KNOW DATE AND REGION OF YOUR TEA

Knowing when your tea was processed is also important because it tells you how much longer the tea has before its quality begins to degrade. Similarly, knowing where your tea comes from may have some significance for you. For instance, as Dragonwell tea increasingly gains in popularity and its price exponentially increases, more regions are starting to plant the Longjing cultivar and process these leaves into teas that resemble Longjing. Although many of these teas are of a very high quality and taste delicious, they are not from the mountains surrounding Hangzhou's famed West Lake—the birthplace of Longjing. Just like the wine world, there are certain teas that are revered not just because of the cultivars or processing used to create the tea but also because of where the plants grew. In this way, the prestige of the tea does not lie in its taste, aroma, or appearance but simply in its rarity. If you seek a specialized tea, you might find yourself interested in trying such a tea from the village with which it gained its popularity so that you can experience why the tea is so "famous."

Picking tea is incredibly labor intensive, primarily because of the large number of leaves needed to make a cup of tea. Although the number of leaves a person can pluck depends on the size of the leaf, a competent plucker can pluck approximately 30,000 tea shoots in a day. Because it takes approximately 3,200 shoots to make a pound of tea, a competent tea plucker can pluck nearly 10 pounds of raw material every day. After processing, however, those leaves are reduced down to just about 2 pounds of tea.

SENSING TEA

Taste buds, through their interaction with various molecules and ions, can differentiate between five taste sensations: saltiness, bitterness, sweetness, sourness, and umami. Tea, in one form or another, can trigger all five of these taste sensations.

Until recently, tea tasters described the taste of tea based on the balance between the five sensations, prizing teas that had a complexity of sensation but not one overpowering taste. Traditionally, the Chinese adopted a language in which they described tea simply by bifurcating between saltiness and sweetness and commenting on how well these two sensations balanced for a particular tea. The more balance, the better tasting. This system has a certain appeal, as it simplifies what one looks for when tasting tea.

As it turns out, this simple system of analyzing the balance between a tea's sweetness and saltiness corresponds to the physiology of our taste buds. Sweet, umami, and bitter tastes are triggered by the binding of molecules to receptors on the cell membranes of our taste buds, whereas saltiness and sourness are perceived when alkali metals or hydrogen ions trigger the taste buds. That is to say, there are essentially two physiological phenomena that take place in our mouth to create tastes. Saltiness and sweetness each trigger a different phenomenon.

As specialty tea gains in popularity throughout North America, tea companies are co-opting marketing language used in other food and drink industries in lieu of a more direct description of tea's taste. Some tea companies now market their teas by describing the flavor profiles of their various teas. Similar to how sommeliers might talk about wine, tea merchants are describing teas through reference to other food items. For example, an oolong tea is less likely to be sold based on the date it was picked, the master who rolled the tea, the area from which the leaves were plucked, or even on how salty or sweet it is, but by the fact that it tastes of "cinnamon, wildflowers, and honey."

On one hand, this movement seems to be taking a lot of the romance out of drinking tea. Instead of simply enjoying the tea for what it is, we are now starting to dissect that enjoyment, breaking it down into subcomponents. No longer is the pleasure of drinking tea simply the joy we feel; the pleasure is now found in dissecting and analyzing our experiences.

Regardless of the psychological effects of modern marketing strategies, there are important physiological reasons why we can experience teas as they relate to other foods. The five sensations only partially contribute to how we taste food. In addition to the five sensations, we also experience flavor through our nose, textures, and temperatures.

Of these three physiological effects, smell, or olfaction, is the most influential because it has the most powerful effect on our perception of taste. There are two ways we perceive the scent of tea: through our nose (orthonasal olfaction) and through the back of our mouth (retronasal olfaction). Although orthonasal and retronasal olfaction are ways in which we perceive the scent of tea, they both greatly influence our perception of taste. For, once our mind experiences an odor coupled with a taste, it marries these two sensations and they become inextricably linked. This influence between retronasal and orthonasal olfaction on our perception of taste is so strong that our mind simply believes that the odors are located in our mouth. Our mind is deceived into

believing that the odors are not just a smell but actually the taste. This deception is referred to as the olfactory referral illusion, and the olfactory referral illusion is why we often speak of teas "tasting" other than through our five taste sensations.

To demonstrate this phenomenon, hold your nose and chew a flavored candy. You should detect the candy's sweetness and its texture. But, you will not notice any of the candy's odor and, therefore, you will not taste any of its flavor. If you let go of your nose, however, the odor molecules from the candy will travel through both your nasal cavity and the back of your throat and you will suddenly "taste" the flavor. In fact, you may find that this sensation is so strong that if you again hold your nose, you will continue to experience the taste because your mind has linked the sweet sensation of the candy with its odor and created one unified taste.
It is for this reason that smelling your cup of tea is absolutely fundamental to the enjoyment of that tea. Only after savoring the tea's aroma, feeling its warmth, and allowing your mind to connect the tea's aroma with its taste can you truly understand and enjoy a cup of tea. Enjoying tea in this way, however, is not conducive to a tea ordered at a fast-food establishment or while driving down the highway, but that's a topic for another book.

CREATING THE PERFECT CUP OF TEA

WATER TEMPERATURE

It is difficult to read a book about tea and not read the instructions couched in the now famously cryptic Chinese instructions for water temperature: "Do not boil the water too hastily, as first it begins to sparkle like crab's eyes, then like fish's eyes, and lastly it boils up like pearls innumerable, spinning and waving about."

Temperature! It can affect the way a tea is processed, the way that it tastes, and the way that it smells. Yet, even with the importance of temperature for the enjoyment of tea, if you put ten tea drinkers in a room, you will likely get ten different opinions as to the best temperatures for steeping tea. Further complicating the issue is the psychological phenomenon known as the confirmation bias, which provides that our opinions are not the result of years of rational, objective analysis but instead solidify from years of noticing only the information that confirms our original beliefs. In other words, once we form our opinions about the proper temperature for steeping tea, we spend the rest of our lives reassuring ourselves that we are correct!

The English and most of the people in the old English Commonwealth states swear that to make a proper cup of tea you must not only use boiling water—you must use rolling, boiling water. The Chinese rarely cite specific water temperatures for making tea, believing that no one temperature is suitable for multiple teas and believing that the proper temperature can only be found after many experiments and tests with each particular tea. With that said, the Chinese unequivocally state, with equal emotive strength as the English have regarding boiling water, that you should never, under any circumstances, drink cold tea. In fact, the Chinese are raised to believe that "cooling tea is perfection, but cold tea is a sin." Americans, on the other hand, usually do not use moral imperatives when discussing the preferred water temperature for making tea, but they certainly do love their cold, sweet, tea.

GENERAL

For whatever it is worth, I side with the Chinese in the great temperature debate. In my experience, variations in water temperatures cause great changes in the taste and aroma of a tea. The more that I drink a particular tea, the more I become aware whether the tea is best suited for warmer or cooler water and then make adjustments accordingly. Plus, science is on the side of the Chinese.

The cause of a tea's bitterness and astringency is based on the chemicals in the leaf. Green, white, and yellow teas have a particular bitterness and astringency due to the teas' high tannin content, chemicals that taste bitter and feel astringent. (Yellow tea tastes sweeter because these tannins degrade during yellow tea's unique non-enzymatic oxidation process.) As discussed in "Changes to Chemical Composition," during the oxidation process, tannins (catechins) are transformed into theaflavins, which have their own unique bitter taste; the difference in bitterness between tannins and theaflavins can only be understood by tasting a black tea and comparing it to the taste of a green tea.

Tannins and theaflavins react with heat differently. As a general rule, teas with more catechins (teas that underwent slight to no oxidation) taste better when steeped with cooler water, whereas teas with higher levels of theaflavins (teas that underwent greater oxidation) are best steeped with warmer water—the warmer water allows these teas to better develop their aromas.

GUIDELINES

With all of this in mind, when I sit to drink a tea for the first time, I rely on the following baseline guide for where to start playing with my teas. These "rules" should only be considered a baseline.

Green, white, and yellow tea: water temperature of 160°F–175°F (71°C–79°C)
Oolong: 180°F–190°F (82°C–88°C)
Black: 195°F–205°F (91°C–96°C)
Dark: 200°F–210°F (93°C–99°C)

QUANTITY

Robert Fortune is known as the English botanist who, while employed by the East India Company, stole Chinese tea plants and helped transform the world's tea market.

At the time of his espionage, the English held a longstanding rule that suggested the use of 1 teaspoon (2 g) of tea leaves for every 6 ounces (175 ml) of water used (1 teacup). In fact, this was such the standard that the English still use a utensil called the teaspoon to help English families make this measurement. Interestingly, as late as the 1800s, most tea sold in the West was reportedly of very poor quality and contained as many twigs and stems as tea leaves. Therefore, the long-held belief that one teaspoon is an appropriate standard of measurement for tea should probably be reconsidered.

Today, we have access to hundreds of teas of all different shapes and sizes, from the small tender leaves of the Silver Needle white tea to the very large leaves of the Taiwanese oolong teas. A teaspoon of Silver Needle and a teaspoon of a Taiwanese oolong tea will certainly contain drastically different amounts of tea matter. For this reason, it is advisable to use tea based on weight and not volume.

There has recently emerged an understanding that over the last few hundred years, the world created two different styles of steeping: the Western style and the Eastern style. For each of these styles, there are different benchmark standards for the amount of tea to use for steeping. The Western style uses lesser amounts of tea and longer steeping times, whereas the Eastern style uses greater amounts of tea and shorter steeping times. Below are the baseline standards.

WESTERN-STYLE STEEPING

1 to 3 grams of tea per 6 to 8 ounces (175 to 235 ml) of water

Initially steep the tea for 2½ to 3 minutes. For each subsequent steeping, increase your steeping time by 30 seconds.

EASTERN-STYLE STEEPING

3 to 6 grams of tea per 4 to 6 ounces (120 to 175 ml) of water

Initially steep the leaves for 12 to 20 seconds. For each subsequent steeping, increase the steeping time by 5 to 10 seconds.

PROCESS FOR MAKING TEA

Regardless of whether you perform a Japanese tea ceremony, serve tea in a diner, or prepare the finest Chinese Da Hong Pao oolong tea, the process of brewing the tea will generally be the same. The next section scrutinizes the processes, equipment, and issues that you may want to consider when trying to enhance the quality and taste of your tea.

1.

2.

3.

QUICK GUIDE

Below are five quick and easy steps that you can follow to maximize the taste of your tea.

1. WARMING VESSELS

Before steeping your tea, warm all the brewing and drinking vessels. Doing so not only cleans the vessels but also warms them so that the water temperature does not significantly decrease when you pour the water into the brewing vessel or when you pour the tea into the drinking vessels.

2. ADDING LEAVES

Consider whether you intend to add the tea leaves to your brewing vessel with your hands, a spoon, or a special utensil. Be sure you have the instruments available.

4.

3. BLANCHING

Pour water on your leaves and then quickly pour out this water. Blanching the leaves not only cleans them, but it also allows them to begin unrolling so that you can maximize your infusion. It is advisable that when you pour out the liquor from the initial blanching that you pour it into your drinking vessels (and then pour out from the drinking vessels). Doing so not only keeps these vessels warm, but it also guarantees that the vessels smell and taste like the tea you are preparing.

4. STEEPING

After blanching the leaves, pour hot water on the leaves and begin the steeping process. If you are steeping the leaves in a container with a top, you may want to pour hot water on the outside of the vessel to keep the vessel warm to protect the water's temperature from decreasing while the leaves are steeping.

5. DECANTING

After you finish steeping your tea for the desired amount of time and at the desired temperature, decant the tea by pouring it into another container. Decanting the tea guarantees that the tea liquor is homogenous and that all samples of the tea taste the same.

SPECIFIC METHODS OF TEA PREPARATION

BRITISH/DUTCH TEA

Most houses in the West have a traditional British- or Dutch-style teapot with a spout and a handle. To optimize the use of this style of teapot, there are a few simple steps you should consider.

To begin, warm the teapot by filling it with hot water.

Discard the warm water and add the tea leaves.

Pour pre-heated water over the leaves. If your teapot has an infuser basket or a strainer, make sure that it is big enough to allow the leaves to expand.

Let the leaves steep in the water. For bigger teapots, this steeping time can be 3 to 5 minutes.

Stop the steeping by pouring the tea into another vessel or by removing the leaves from the tea.

Serve and enjoy.

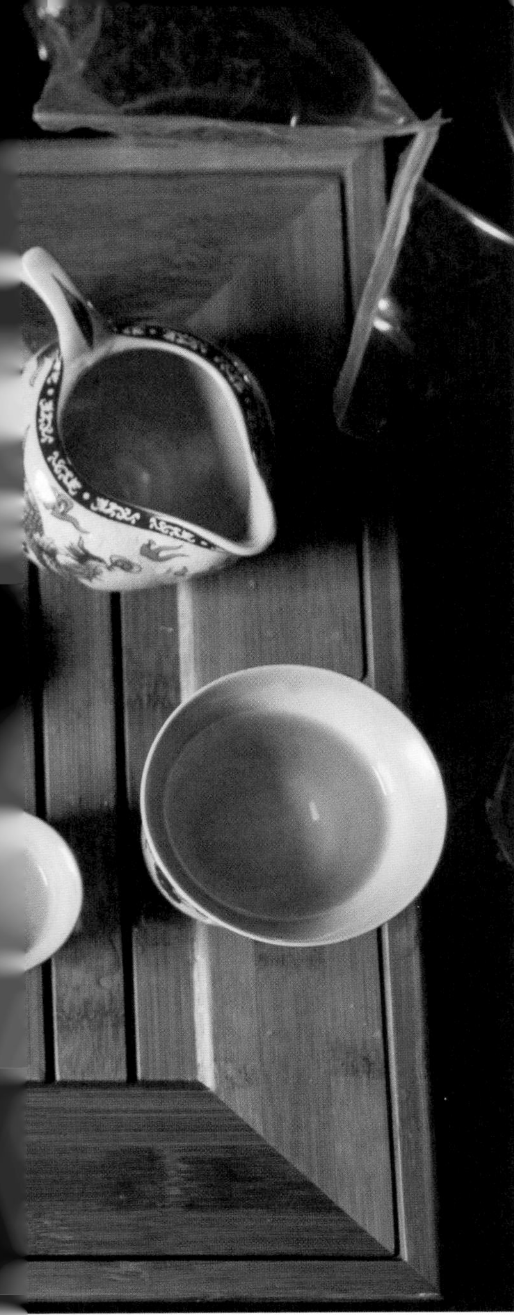

GUNG FU CHA

Spend time with serious tea drinkers and you will invariably hear them talk about steeping tea Gung Fu Cha style. This style of steeping tea refers to the way tea is steeped in China and Taiwan when there is a desire for a more formal preparation for tea. Although it is not nearly as ritualistic as the Japanese Chanoyu tea ceremony, such preparation requires a relatively formal series of steps. This method of steeping tea usually uses a Yixing pot (page 84), although a gaiwan (page 83) works too.

To begin, warm all of the vessels with boiling water. The boiling water not only warms the vessels, but it also partially sterilizes and cleans them. The water from this stage is discarded. It is common in southern China and Taiwan to use tweezers when touching the teacups.

Measure and then display the tea leaves so everyone can appreciate their look, shape, and color.

Fill the teapot with the appropriate amount of tea leaves. Unlike the more generic recommendations listed above for ratios of leaves to water, Gung Fu Cha requires a high concentration of tea leaves to water (as much as 10 to 15 grams of tea for a small [150 ml] Yixing pot, although 5 grams of tea for a medium-sized gaiwan is usually sufficient).

Pour hot water on the tea leaves. Customarily this initial rinse is poured from an elevated pot and with enough water so that the water overflows the pot, allowing the leaves to tumble.

Immediately pour the tea from this steeping into the teacups. This tea is not consumed and is used only to warm and rinse the teacups. This step also imbues the teacups with the taste and aroma of the tea being prepared.

Again fill the teapot with hot water. This time, the water is poured from a much lower level and the teapot is filled only until the water reaches the pot's mouth. Place the lid back on top of the teapot and pour the tea from the initial steeping on the teapot to keep the outside of the pot warm. Allow the tea to steep for 10 to 20 seconds.

Filter the tea into a tea pitcher, which is used to fill the teacups.

Repeat these steps an additional four to eight times, or more as desired.

After the preparation is completed, carefully remove the leaves from the pot and display them for everyone's appreciation.

SENCHADO

Japanese tea culture is inextricably linked with the highly formalized and almost religious ceremony known as Chanoyu. Because the intricacies of Chanoyu are great enough for an entire book, in this book I only outline Senchado, Japan's more informal method of preparing tea. The Senchado method of tea preparation is rooted in traditional Chinese methods of tea preparation and, therefore, is very similar to the Chinese Gung Fu Cha. The biggest difference between these two methods is that Senchado generally only uses the famous Japanese green tea, Gyokuro, and the famous Japanese teapot, the kyusu.

To begin, warm all of the vessels with boiling water.

Place 1 to 2 heaping teaspoons (2 to 4 g) of green, white, or yellow tea into the kyusu.

Pour warm water into the kyusu. (Although each tea will taste best at a different temperature, the water should be 150°F–170°F, or 66°C–77°C.)

Steep for 30 seconds.

Pour equal amounts of tea directly from the kyusu into the teacups. It is a good practice to fill each teacup halfway and then continue to add to each cup until all the tea has been used. This guarantees that each cup will have the same amount of tea. Be sure to use all the tea so that the tea leaves do not continue to steep.

Smell the tea.

Drink the tea.

Repeat.

RETURNING CRAFT TO TEA CULTURE

The twentieth century was the century of tea commodification. In less than one hundred years, the tea industry went from one that sold primarily single-estate, hand-rolled, loose-leaf tea to one that primarily sold premade tea in plastic bottles as well as tea dust mixed with dried herbs and spices in paper tea bags. According to the Tea Association of the USA, of all the tea consumed in the United States, 65 percent is consumed from tea made with tea bags; 25 percent is ready-to-drink tea (tea in a bottle) and iced-tea mixes; and 5 percent is made from instant tea powder and loose-leaf tea. This is a far cry from what Americans were drinking as recently as the late 1800s and first quarter of the 1900s.

Lost in the clutter of these iced-tea bottles, instant tea powder, bleached paper bags, tisanes, and their corresponding marketing regimes are the traditions and techniques that defined the world's great tea cultures. In my journeys around the world over the past twenty-plus years, I have experienced and collected many of these influential traditions and techniques and have shared them in the following sections.

SERVES FOUR

INGREDIENTS

- 4 cups (946 ml) water
- 2 to 3 teaspoons (4 to 6 g) loose black tea, preferably Ceylon, Assam, or Nilgiri
- Cream (to taste)
- Sugar (to taste)

ENGLISH "CUPPA" AND DUTCH TEA

The English and Dutch introduced tea to the Western world just over four hundred years ago. In those four hundred years, they created a virtual monopoly on how tea is prepared and consumed in the West.

Whether the English and Dutch style of tea preparation is the "best" style is usually not an issue of debate, because most people in Western countries believe their style of preparation is the only way tea should be made and the only way tea should taste. The style of tea preparation introduced by the English and Dutch forgoes much of tea's complexities in preference of creating a rich, full-bodied, black tea. The preparation also creates a rather bitter and bold tea. So, cream and sugar become almost essential. With that being said, there is something incredible about a strong, malty black tea perfected by a dash of cream and a touch of sugar.

Bring your water to a roiling boil and fill the pot with 2 cups (475 ml) water. After sufficiently warming the pot, discard the water and place 2 to 3 teaspoons loose black tea, preferably an Indian Assam black tea or a derivative of Assam such as English Breakfast or Earl Grey, into the pot. Add the remaining 2 cups (475 ml) boiling water into the pot with the tea leaves. Allow to steep for 5 minutes. Filter into 2 teacups. Add ¼ cup (60 ml) cream and 1 to 2 teaspoons (4 to 9 g) sugar per cup. Enjoy.

According to Kate Fox in her book *Watching the English: The Hidden Rules of English Behaviour*, "taking sugar in your tea is regarded by many as an infallible lower-class indicator: even one spoonful is a bit suspect . . . more than one and you are lower middle at best; more than two and you are definitely working class." Other social taboos for the English are to stir too noisily and to put milk in your cup before the tea, as both acts apparently are indicators of a lower social status.

RUSSIAN TEA

SERVES FOUR

INGREDIENTS

- 4 cups (946 ml) water for steeping
- 4 cups (946 ml) water for serving
- ¼ to ⅓ cup (24 to 32 g) loose black tea, preferably CTC Assam or strong Chinese black tea
- Cubed sugar (served on the side)

Unlike the English and Dutch, who imported their teas via ship, Russia imported much of its tea via caravan traveling overland through central Asia.

The dry and often cold climate of central Asia was much more conducive to transporting tea safely. Therefore, when tea arrived in St. Petersburg or Moscow, its quality was generally much better than the quality found from the English and Dutch merchants, giving the Russians a reputation (which many still hold today) of having the best quality tea in Europe. As Russia's political power increased in the 1800s and 1900s, they had a great influence on the way in which eastern Europeans and many people living in the Middle East drank tea.

The Russian style of tea preparation requires that a very strong tea concentrate, which is repeatedly diluted with hot water and sugar. A concentrate allows each tea drinker to dilute the tea to his or her own liking.

Bring 8 cups (1.9 L) water to a rolling boil. Place tea into a small pot. Add 4 cups (946 ml) boiling water into the pot with the tea. Cover and simmer for 20 minutes. When the tea becomes very strong, filter the tea concentrate into a teapot with a spout. Fill teacups one-quarter to one-half full with the tea concentrate and then fill each teacup with boiling water. Serve with cubed sugar on the side. Refill the teacups with tea concentrate and water as needed.

The Russian style of tea preparation is easiest using a classic Russian samovar. A samovar is designed so that the teapot containing the tea concentrate sits on top of a large cylinder of boiling water, much like a double boiler. The steam from the boiling water in the cylinder not only heats the tea concentrate but is used to dilute the tea concentrate, which is easily done via a tap at the base of the cylinder.

SERVES FOUR

INGREDIENTS

- 4 cups (946 ml) water for steeping
- 4 cups (946 ml) water for serving
- ⅓ cup (32 g) black tea leaves, preferably a CTC Assam or Ceylon black tea
- Cubed sugar (served on the side)

TURKISH TEA

Tea in Turkey is very much a ritual. I was first exposed to this fine tradition while living in Urumqi, China, in western China with the Turkic group called the Uyghurs.

As the main trading center between Turkey and China, Urumqi was a magnet for Turkish businessmen and, therefore, Turkish tea. Participating in the Turkic tea traditions in China certainly illuminated how disparate the world treats tea.

This style of tea preparation is very close to the Russian traditions with one very important difference. The Turks leave their tea leaves steeping in the tea concentrate and will filter the tea when the concentrate is poured into the cup. The Russians, on the other hand, filter the concentrate into the warm pot of the samovar. By allowing the leaves to steep continuously, the Turks create an extremely bitter and astringent tea concentrate, much more pungent than the traditional Russian tea.

Fill a medium pot with 8 cups (1.9 L) water and bring to a boil. In a fine-mesh filter, quickly rinse the leaves with cold water and allow to drain. Place the washed tea leaves in a small pot and add 4 cups (946 ml) boiling water. Allow the leaves to steep 10 to 20 minutes or until the tea concentrate becomes very bitter and strong. When the tea finishes steeping, fill the teacups halfway with the tea concentrate. Use the remaining 4 cups (946 ml) boiling water to fill the cups. Serve with cubed sugar on the side. While drinking tea, create a double boiler by placing the small pot with the tea concentrate into the medium pot with the remaining boiling water, simmer, and cover. When you need to refill the teacups, repeat the process until you are out of concentrate or finished drinking tea.

Every region of Morocco and North Africa prepares tea slightly differently. Some regions add wormwood leaves or lemon verbena with the mint. To try this, simply add ¼ to ½ tablespoon (1.5 to 3 g) of lemon verbena to the tea at the same time that you add the mint, or you can add the lemon verbena in lieu of mint.

SERVES FOUR

INGREDIENTS

- 4 cups (946 ml) boiling water
- 2 teaspoons (4 g) gunpowder green tea
- 4 teaspoons (18 g) sugar
- 1 bunch mint

MOROCCAN TEA (NORTH AFRICAN GREEN TEA)

The people of Morocco started drinking tea after English traders introduced the beverage to the North Africans during the countries' trade boom in the eighteenth century.

Today most, if not all, of North Africa has adopted the Moroccan preferences for very strong green tea infused with bunches of mint and piles of sugar. The Moroccan tradition is so beloved that you now see minority groups as far east as western China infusing their teas with mint and sugar, forgoing the Chinese tradition of drinking unaltered pure tea.

Bring 4 cups (946 ml) water to a boil. Place gunpowder green tea into a small pot. For every 2 teaspoons of gunpowder green tea you added to the small pot, add 2 cups (475 ml) boiling water and allow to steep for at least 15 minutes. Do not stir! Filter the tea into a clean pot and add sugar (approximately 4 teaspoons, or 18 g, for every cup of tea). Cover the tea and bring the sweet tea to a boil. Allow to boil for 3 to 5 minutes. Remove the tea from the heat and add whole mint (approximately ¼ to ½ cup, or 24 to 48 g, of whole mint per cup of tea). Allow the mint to infuse for 2 minutes and then remove. (Many Moroccans will remove the mint within 2 minutes after infusion, believing that having too much mint will cause acid reflux.)

The term gunpowder is thought to come from the English who thought that the ball shape of the tea was reminiscent of black gunpowder. Gunpowder is traditionally made from a green tea process via the steaming method. The tea is rolled into small balls and, therefore, experiences less damage during transit. Because gunpowder green tea is generally steamed and retains much of its flavor and aroma due to the protection it receives from its shape, this tea is known for having a very strong "green" flavor and smell.

SERVES SIX

PERSIAN ROSE TEA

If you carefully document the tea-drinking habits of people around the world, you will uncover the trading patterns of the past two hundred years.

INGREDIENTS

- 6 cups (1.4 L) water
- 6 green cardamom pods, crushed
- 1 tablespoon (13 g) sugar
- 2 teaspoons (4 g) black tea
- Rose water (to taste)
- Mint (served on the side)

Every style of tea preparation reveals not only the taste preferences of the locals but also the products traded between various regions of the world. This phenomenon is best explained by the Persian/Iranian classic cardamom rose tea. Sandwiched between Russia and India, this recipe is clearly influenced by both great cultures while also demonstrating the Persians' unique appreciation of the subtle taste of rose.

Bring water, cardamom pods, and sugar to a boil in a medium saucepan. Reduce heat to low. After sugar fully dissolves, add tea. Simmer 3 minutes and add rose water to taste. Serve with fresh mint.

Many gourmet grocery stores now carry rose water. Making your own rose water, however, is relatively easy and more delicious than any premade concoction. The following is how I make rose water:

1. Pick the rose petals after all dew has evaporated. Use only the flower's petals, not the stem or leaves.
2. Thoroughly wash the petals.
3. Place the rose petals in a large pot and add just enough water to cover the petals. Simmer covered over low heat (the water should be steaming but not boiling). Allow the water to simmer until the petals have lost their color and the water has taken on the color of the rose petals. You will see the rose oil floating on the surface.
4. Strain the water and collect in a container. Store in a refrigerator.

IMPORTANT: The petals must be freshly picked and free of pesticides or other chemicals. If you cannot grow your own roses for your rose water, find a friend or farmer who can verify that the roses are free of chemicals.

If you do not have access to all the required ingredients, you can still make a delicious masala chai. The most important ingredients, other than milk, water, and tea, are cardamom, cinnamon, and clove. These three spices represent the base spice mix for virtually all masala chai recipes and can be used alone in the quantities suggested to make a quality masala chai.

SERVES TWO

INDIAN SPICED TEA

Undeniably, the world has recently acquired a taste for the milky-smooth spiced tea drink of south Asia called masala chai (often redundantly named *masala chai tea*). This phenomenon is remarkable considering that the people of the Indian subcontinent themselves have only been drinking tea for about one hundred years. Yet, even with their relatively short tea-drinking history, south Asians, as much as anyone else in the world, have integrated tea into their own unique culture. In fact, tea is so integral to the south Asian culture that it is impossible to talk about one without talking about the other. No matter whom you ask throughout south Asia, everyone has an irrationally strong opinion as to who makes the best masala chai—their answer is invariably their own mother!

As such, one of the privileges of being married into a south Asian family is that I have collected the proprietary recipes and techniques used by in-laws in making their masala chai. The following recipe represents a collection of my family's recipes and techniques pieced together over the years through various trips to India, and through my incessant need to hide in kitchens and take notes of how to prepare an outstanding masala chai.

INGREDIENTS

- 2 cups (475 ml) water
- 2 cups (475 ml) milk
- 6 to 8 green cardamom pods, crushed
- 8 to 10 black peppercorns
- 1 cinnamon stick, broken
- 1 teaspoon fennel seeds
- 1 teaspoon ground clove
- 1 star anise
- 1 teaspoon finely grated fresh ginger
- 4 teaspoons (8 g) loose black tea (Assam)
- Sugar or honey (to taste)

Bring the water, milk, cardamom pods, peppercorns, cinnamon stick, fennel seeds, clove, star anise, and fresh ginger to a boil in a medium saucepan. Lower the heat and simmer 2 to 3 minutes or until you achieve your desired taste. Remove the saucepan from the heat and add the black tea. Steep the tea for 3 to 4 minutes. Strain the masala chai into a clean saucepan or into four cups and add sugar or honey to taste.

TECHNIQUE

After the tea has steeped and the sugar is added, I boil the masala chai four times; I do this carefully because the masala chai has a habit of overflowing. When the masala chai comes to a boil, I remove it from the heat, let the foam subside, and then repeat three times. Doing so caramelizes the sugars and adds a lovely taste to the masala chai. I also "pull" the masala chai tea by pouring it 2 to 3 feet (61 to 91 cm) from one saucepan into another. By doing this four or five times, I not only cool the tea, but I also aerate it to give it a more full mouthfeel.

To find the required ingredients, consider shopping at a local Indian/Pakistani/Bangladeshi grocery store. These stores will have all the spices that you need at a very reasonable price. In fact, after shopping at these stores, you may find yourself asking why you would ever buy spices anywhere else!

HYDERABAD IRANIAN TEA

SERVES ONE

Although tea has been in India for just over one hundred years, some interesting techniques for tea preparation have emerged from this subcontinent.

Many of these traditions come from India's unique geographical location and the cultures surrounding the subcontinent. Hyderabad's Iranian chai is one of these traditions. About one hundred years ago, Persian traders settled in the southern city of Hyderabad and brought an entirely new way of making tea. Today, Hyderabad's tea scene is synonymous with Iranian chai.

What is fascinating about Hyderabad's Iranian tea is the fact that the only difference between Iranian chai and English tea is the way that it is processed. Like the Russians and Turks, the Persians/Iranians drink very strong tea. Traditionally, to offset the bitterness and astringency of this strong tea, a person would tuck a sugar cube in a cheek and sip the highly concentrated tea through that sugar cube. The sugar cut the bitterness and astringency. Wanting to fit in with the locals, the Persians added milk and sugar and the rest, as they say, is history.

INGREDIENTS

- 1½ cups (355 ml) water
- 2 teaspoons (4 g) loose black tea
- 2 cups (475 ml) milk
- 2 to 3 teaspoons (9 to 14 g) sugar
- 1 or 2 crushed cardamom pods (optional)

Put water and tea into a small saucepan, cover, and bring to a boil. Reduce temperature and let simmer for 15 to 20 minutes. (In Hyderabad, chai wallahs will simmer their tea for hours to create a very strong tea. Consider experimenting with making stronger tea concentrates.) Heat the milk and sugar in a small saucepan over low heat. Simmer the sweet milk for 20 to 60 minutes, stirring occasionally. (Similar to the tea, the longer you allow the milk to simmer the better. You want the milk to become thick and rich.) Once your tea concentrate and milk syrup are finished, add the milk to the tea in the ratio of one-quarter tea to three-quarters milk. If you want to add cardamom, add the cardamom to the milk syrup as it simmers.

Facing cutting line
36
Center back seamline
Top-stitching line
Straight of grain
36
36

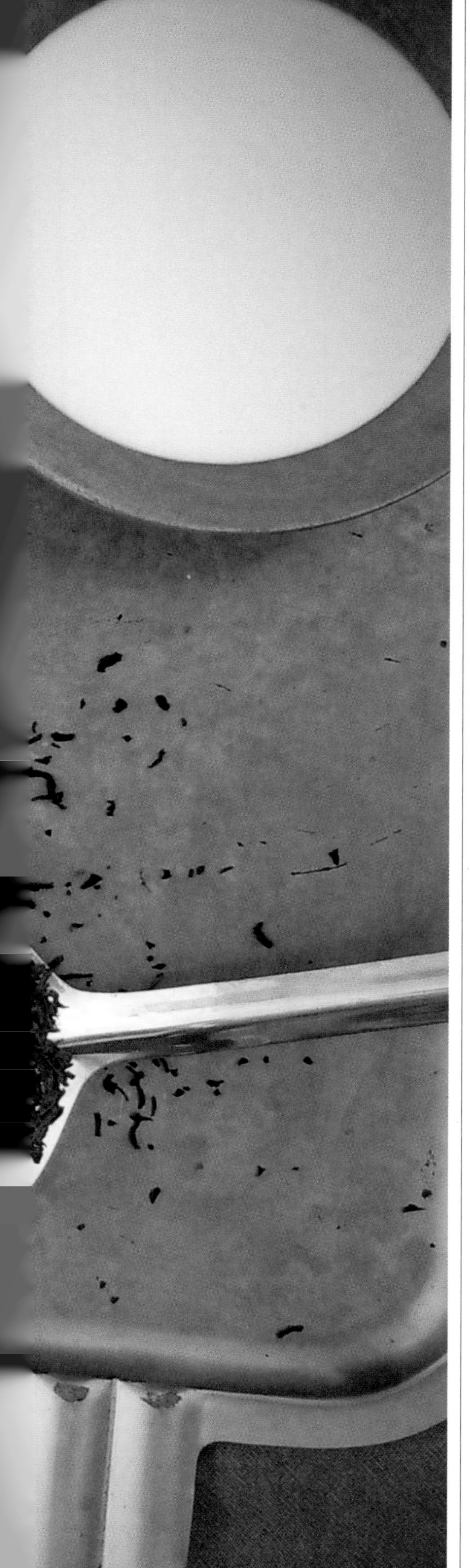

SERVES TWO

SOUTH INDIAN BLACK CARDAMOM TEA

INGREDIENTS

- 2 cups (475 ml) water
- 2 cardamom pods, broken
- 2 teaspoons (4 g) fennel
- 2 teaspoons (4 g) loose black tea
- 1 cup (235 ml) milk
- Sugar or honey (to taste)

In the West, we often use masala chai as if these two words designate a very specific type of drink, like the aforementioned cardamom rose tea. Most do not realize that masala chai actually means "spiced tea" and refers not to a specific tea but to a general group of teas. As one can imagine, there are as many variations of masala chai as there are spices in India.

The following masala chai is a very typical style of tea made throughout the southern states of India. Because it includes tea, it beautifully demonstrates how the people of south Asia incorporated tea into their more traditional beverage. This tea is an adaptation of a drink families historically gave their children when they felt sick. I love the tea because the black cardamom adds sensuality by providing a smoky taste and aroma that is not found in more traditional masala chai recipes.

Bring water, cardamom pods, and fennel to a boil in a medium saucepan. Cover and simmer until 1 cup (235 ml) liquid remains. Remove from heat and add tea. Steep for 3 minutes. Add milk. Return to heat and bring to a boil. Boil for 2 to 3 minutes and then strain into 2 teacups. Add sugar or honey to taste.

SERVES FOUR

ETHIOPIAN TEA

Although this book is dedicated to capital "T" tea and takes a hard-line stance on what should and should not be considered tea, the one exception I make is Ethiopian tea, which is technically a tisane and not a tea (it does not use leaves from the Camellia sinensis plant).

I included this recipe for three reasons. First, it is delicious. Second, the Ethiopians show such generosity and love when sharing this tea that it might as well contain the leaves of the Camellia sinensis plant. And, third, Ethiopian tea demonstrates how trade patterns of the nineteenth and twentieth centuries affected tea traditions around the world.

Ethiopia sits on the western border of the Indian Ocean, directly across from India, and there is a long history of trade, evidenced by Ethiopian tea traditions that are virtually identical to India's classic masala chai. Unlike India, however, Ethiopia was never colonized and, therefore, was never introduced to tea as a tradable commodity. So, today, a traditional Ethiopian tea is similar to a masala chai but without the tea leaves! In other words, it is what Indians would be drinking but for the fact that the English introduced tea to south Asia in the nineteenth and twentieth centuries.

Bring water, cardamom pods, peppercorns, cinnamon stick, fennel seeds, clove, star anise, and fresh ginger to a boil in a medium saucepan. Lower the heat and simmer for 2 to 3 minutes or until you achieve your desired taste. Remove the saucepan from the heat and add the orange zest. Steep the tea for 3 to 4 minutes. Strain the tea into a clean saucepan or into 4 cups and add sugar or honey to taste.

INGREDIENTS

- 4 cups (946 ml) water
- 6 to 8 green cardamom pods (crushed)
- 8 to 10 black peppercorns
- 1 cinnamon stick, broken
- 1 teaspoon fennel seeds
- 1 teaspoon ground clove
- 1 star anise
- 1 teaspoon finely grated fresh ginger
- ½ teaspoon orange zest
- Sugar (to taste)

Many Southeast Asian teas have an unmistakable yet subtle vanilla flavor and taste. To duplicate this flavor and taste, replace the sugar with vanilla sugar.

Ingedients:
2 cups (400 g) granulated sugar
1 vanilla bean, whole

Put the sugar in an airtight container. Slice the vanilla bean vertically with the back of a knife and scrape the seeds into the container with the sugar. Bury the sliced vanilla bean in the sugar and seal tightly. Let the sugar sit for 1 to 2 weeks. Use vanilla sugar as you would regular granulated sugar in any of your tea recipes for a more complex taste.

SERVES FOUR

INGREDIENTS

- 4 cups (946 ml) water
- 4 teaspoons (8 g) loose black tea
- ¾ cup (150 g) sugar
- Ice
- Half-and-half (to fill)

SOUTHEAST ASIAN TEH TARIK TEA

My first introduction to some of the great tea traditions came when I was studying at a college in Malaysia in the early 1990s. There I discovered the great tradition of late-night markets, spicy foods, and deliciously sweet tea: teh tarik! Served hot or cold, this tea is best paired with a spicy noodle or rice dish.

Bring water to a boil in a small pot. Add tea and sugar to another pot. When water is boiling, pour it over the tea and sugar. Gently simmer the tea for 3 minutes and then remove from heat. Steep the tea, off the heat, for an additional 30 minutes. At the end of the 30 minutes, filter the tea concentrate into another container and allow to cool. (This concentrate will last days in your refrigerator).

To make the iced version, fill highball glasses with ice. Then fill each glass three-quarters full with the cooled concentrate and fill the remainder of each glass with half-and-half. (Most of my friends in Malaysia used sweetened condensed milk instead of half-and-half or cream. This makes a very sweet tea, but on a hot humid Malaysian sunny day, nothing really beats it!) When you fill the remainder of the glass with half-and-half or cream, be sure to pour slowly to create the two distinct layers: the tea layer and the cream layer.

TECHNIQUE

If you want to serve or drink your teh tarik warm, do not cool the tea concentrate. Simply add the tea concentrate and the cream together and begin to pull the tea by pouring the tea 2 to 3 feet from one saucepan into another. By doing this four or five times, you not only cool the tea, but you also aerate it to give it a more full mouthfeel. Pour the tea and enjoy.

CONTEMPORARY IDEAS

As people become exposed to tea traditions and techniques, and are more willing to experiment with ingredients, a new outlook on tea is developing. This next section surveys different ways to prepare hot and cold tea, introducing contemporary tastes and sensibilities to the ancient beverage.

ALMOND FENNEL TEA (BADAM CHAI)

INGREDIENTS

- 3 cups (705 ml) water
- 1½ teaspoons (3 g) fennel seeds
- ¼ cup (60 ml) milk
- 2 teaspoons (4 g) loose black tea
- 8 shelled, coarsely broken raw almonds
- Sugar or honey (to taste)

Bring water and fennel seeds to a boil in a medium saucepan. Add milk and reduce heat to low. Let simmer for 2–3 minutes. Remove saucepan from heat, add tea, and steep for 3 minutes. Divide almonds between 2 cups. Strain the tea over the almonds and serve hot with sugar or honey on the side.

SERVES FOUR

BASIL PEACH TEA

INGREDIENTS

- 1 tablespoon (6 g) loose black tea
- 1 cup (40 g) loosely packed fresh basil, plus more for serving
- 4 cups (946 ml) water
- ¼ cup (60 ml) chilled simple syrup (see recipe on page 139)
- 2 peaches, thinly sliced
- Ice

Combine tea and basil in a medium saucepan. Bring water to a boil, remove water from heat, and let sit for 1 minute. Pour the hot water over the tea and basil. Steep for 4 to 5 minutes. Add simple syrup to tea and let cool to room temperature. Discard basil leaves. Place peaches in a pitcher. Pour tea over peaches. Chill. Serve over ice with a fresh sprig of basil.

INGREDIENTS

- 2 cups (475 ml) milk
- 3 cinnamon sticks, plus more for garnish
- 2 teaspoons (4 g) loose black tea
- Honey (to taste)

CINNAMON CREAM TEA

Heat milk with cinnamon sticks in a saucepan until bubbles appear, about 200°F (93°C). Remove from heat and add tea. Steep for 3 to 4 minutes and add honey. Strain into 2 teacups and garnish with clean cinnamon stick.

SERVES FOUR

INGREDIENTS

- 2 cups (475 ml) water
- ½ cup (48 g) chopped fresh mint
- 1 teaspoon crushed fresh ginger
- 2 teaspoons (4 g) loose black tea
- Honey (to taste)

GINGER MINT TEA

Bring water, mint, and ginger to a boil in a medium saucepan. Lower the heat to medium and boil an additional 3–5 minutes. Remove from heat and add tea. Steep for 3 minutes. Strain into cups and, if desired, add honey to taste.

SERVES FIVE

INGREDIENTS

- 5 cups (1.2 L) water
- 1 tablespoon (6 g) loose black tea
- 1 pound (455 g) hulled and quartered strawberries
- ¾ cup (150 g) sugar
- 1 cup (40 g) fresh basil, plus more for garnish

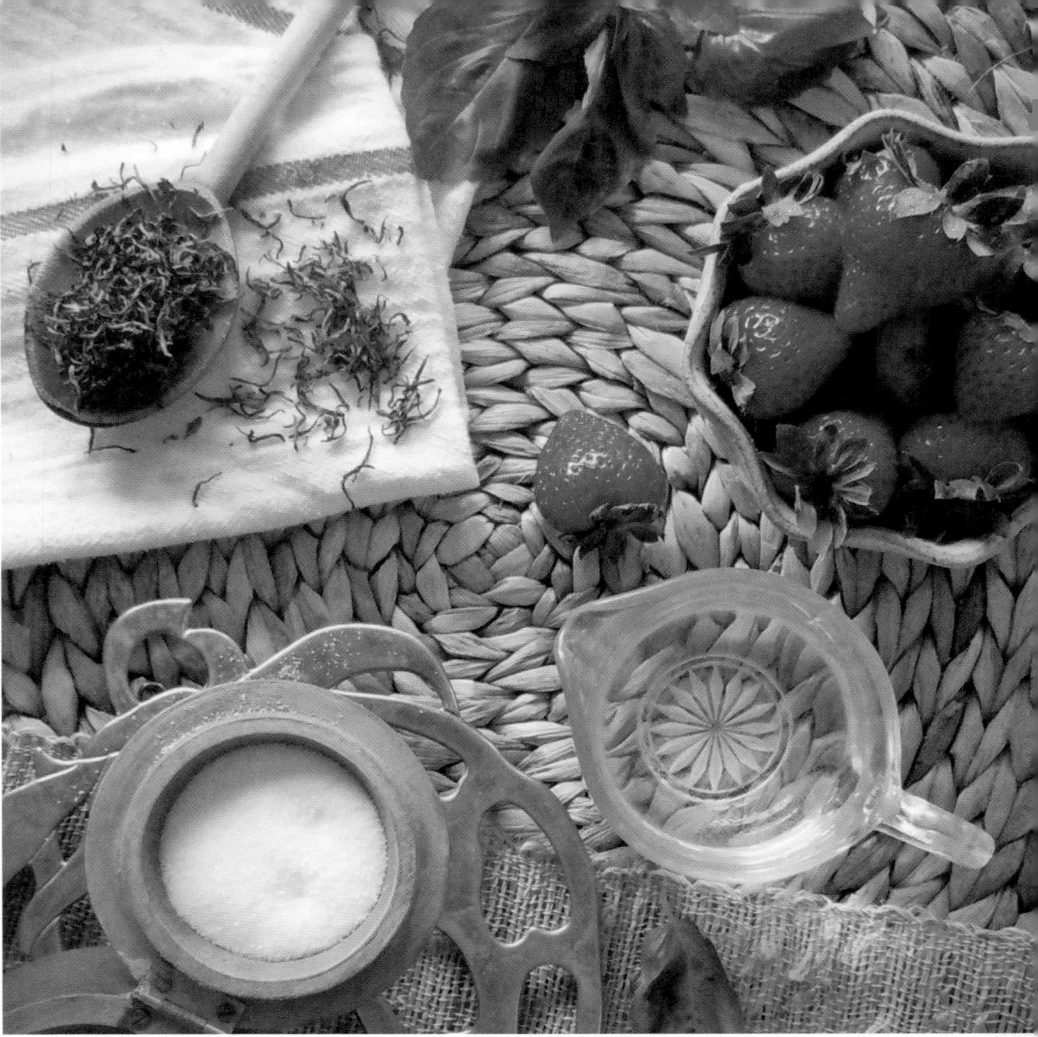

STRAWBERRY-BASIL ICED TEA

Heat 4 cups (946 ml) water until bubbles appear. Remove from heat and add tea. Steep for 4 minutes and strain tea into a pitcher. Place strawberries into a bowl. Heat 1 cup (235 ml) water with sugar until sugar completely dissolves. Remove syrup from heat and add basil. Steep for 10 to 12 minutes. Discard basil. Mix syrup with strawberries. Let cool. Pour strawberry-basil syrup into tea. Refrigerate tea until chilled. Serve over ice and garnish with basil.

SERVES FIVE

WHITE TEA WITH HONEY OR MAPLE SYRUP

INGREDIENTS

- 2 to 3 teaspoons (4 to 6 g) white tea
- 5 cups (1.2 L) water
- Maple syrup or honey (to taste)

Sometimes the simplest changes or additions make an old favorite taste new and exciting. For this white refresher, I like to use Michigan maple syrup or a complex honey such as Acacia honey. I find that the right honey can add a depth often missing from some white teas.

Place white tea in a pot and add 5 cups (1.2 L) warm water (170°F, or 77°C). Allow the tea to steep for 3 minutes. Filter the tea into 2 teacups and add maple syrup.

COLD TEA

Tea is often thought of as a warm, soothing drink. But, tea has a wonderful cold side too. Throughout the world people are more willing to try a cold tea and when they do, they often experience tea in a completely new way. Steeping tea with cold water is a wonderful way to explore a tea because it prohibits many of the leaf's catechins from leaching into the water, creating a tea that is very sweet but without the bitterness or astringency associated with many teas.

SIMPLE COLD-STEEPING TECHNIQUES

Cold-steeping (often called cold-brewing) is perhaps the simplest of all steeping techniques and creates a smooth and naturally sweet tea unlike any teas made with hot water. Although any tea can be prepared via the cold-steeping method, the method allows you to steep the tea leaves only once. Therefore, if you cold-steep an expensive tea, the method will prove to be an expensive method for preparing tea.

To cold-brew tea, place 1 to 1½ teaspoons (2 to 3 g) of loose-leaf tea for every 6 ounces (175 ml) of water into a bowl, bucket, or pitcher and fill the container with room-temperature water. Let the container sit in a cool place for 10 to 12 hours and filter the liquid into a pitcher or other container that will fit in your refrigerator. Cold-steeped tea is most delicious served slightly cold and is often made with a sweetener such as table sugar or honey. When I cold-brew tea, I usually make it before I go to bed so that when I wake the tea is ready.

ICED TEA/ SUN TEA

Throughout the midwest and southern regions of the United States, the most popular way to cold-brew tea is by using the sun. The sun-tea method is virtually identical to the cold-steeping method, but it produces a little more bitterness and astringency (often thought of as "body") because the sun slightly warms the tea and accelerates the steeping time. Instead of steeping the tea for 10 to 12 hours as in the cold-steeping method, you can steep a tea in the sun for as little as 6 to 8 hours. Similar to cold-brewing, sun tea is made with 1 to 1½ teaspoons (2 to 3 g) of tea for every cup (6 ounces, or 175 ml) of water. Put the tea in a clear glass container and fill the container with room-temperature water. Seal the container and place it outside in direct sunlight. When the tea is ready, filter the liquid into a pitcher filled with ice and serve cold with lemon and sugar.

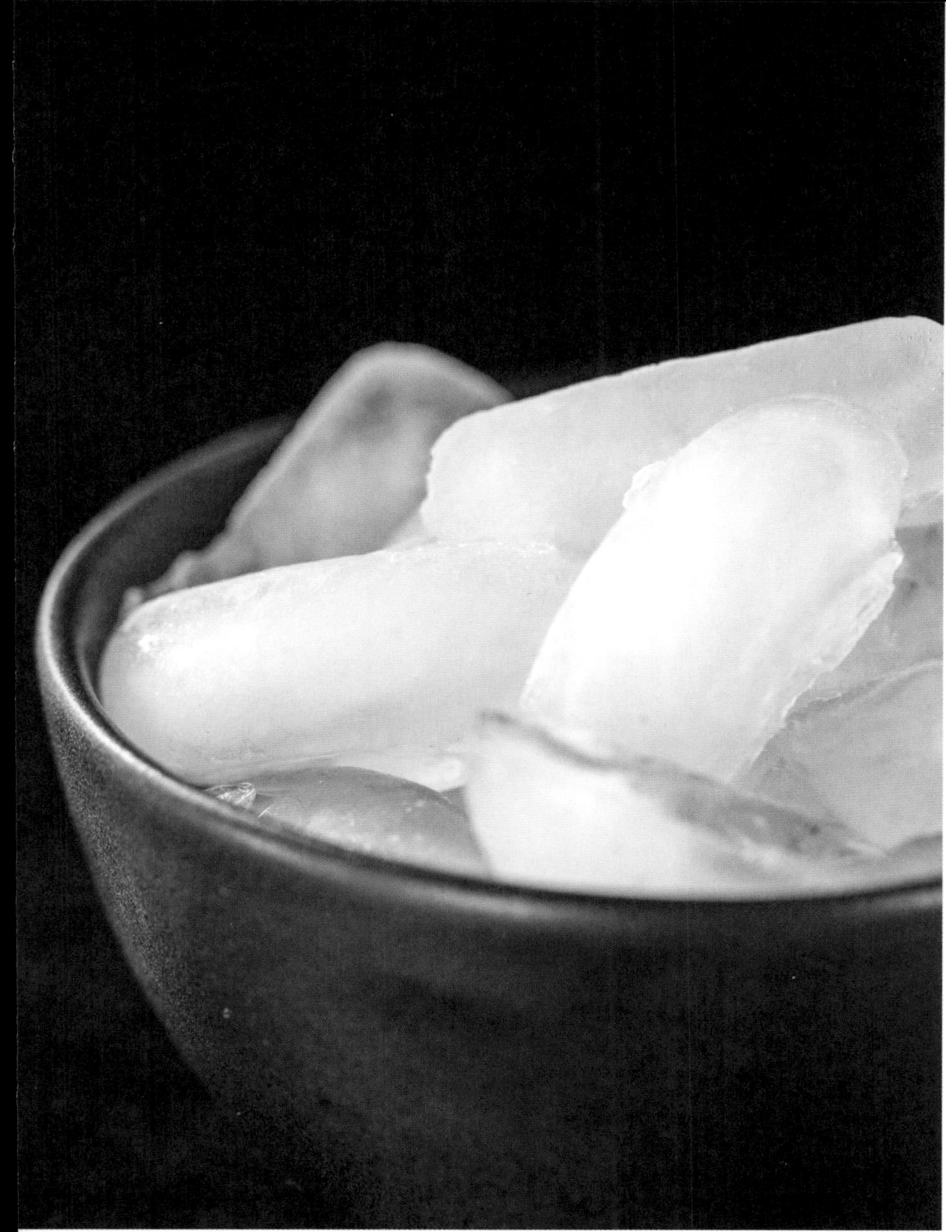

JAPANESE COLD-STEEPED TEA

I recently learned of an interesting method for cold-steeping green tea used by friends in Japan. This Japanese-style cold-steeped tea is perfect for making a cold tea from the grassy green steamed teas of Japan, specifically Sencha. To make a Japanese-style iced tea, put 1 to 2 teaspoons (2 to 3 g) of green tea in a bowl and fill the bowl with ice. When the ice melts, the tea is ready. This method creates a very light and very cold green tea. But, on a hot summer day, it is a wonderful and subtle way to prepare tea.

SERVES TWO

INGREDIENTS

- 2 teaspoons (4 g) black tea
- 2 cups (475 ml) water
- ½ cup (100 g) sugar

SOUTHERN-STYLE SWEET TEA

If you travel to the southern United States, you will surely experience the region's drink: southern-style sweet tea. Those who grew up with this style of tea have a hard time drinking tea any other way, and those who did not grow up drinking tea prepared in this way are often challenged with the taste. Unlike the Russian or English traditions, the southern-style sweet tea is sweet but not strong. In fact, the tea taste is secondary to the sweetness.

Place tea in a small pot. Boil water in another pot. After the water begins to boil, remove the pot from the heat and let the water cool for 1 to 2 minutes. Pour the water on top of the tea leaves in the small pot and let steep for 1 to 2 minutes. Filter the steeped liquid into a clean glass pitcher and add sugar. Fill the pitcher with ice and let cool. Serve with a slice of lemon and enjoy. The tea can be refrigerated for several days.

SERVES ONE

SIMPLE SYRUPS AND INFUSIONS

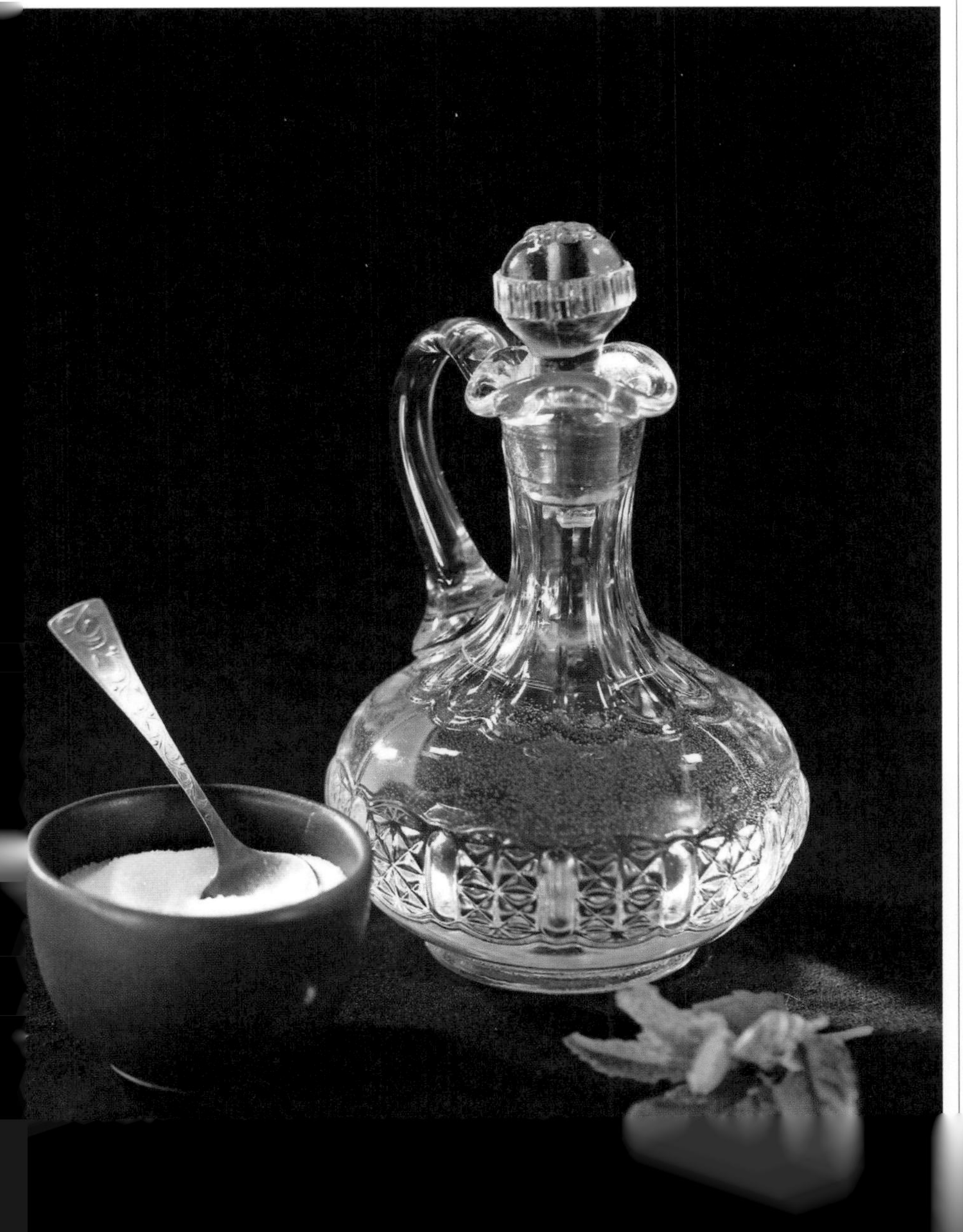

INGREDIENTS

1 cup (235 ml) water

1 cup (200 g) sugar

A disadvantage in cold-steeping tea is that it is difficult to sweeten the tea because it is hard to dissolve the sugar or honey. The best means for sweetening a cold-steeped tea is to make a simple syrup that is added after the tea steeps.

Combine the water and sugar in a pot and warm gently over medium-low heat. Stirring constantly, remove the pot from the heat as soon as the sugar dissolves. Let cool and pour into a container from which you can pour. The simple syrup can be refrigerated for up to 2 weeks.

To flavor my cold-steeped teas, I infuse the flavor into my simple syrup. So, if I want a mint-flavored cold-steeped tea, I place a bunch of mint into the simple syrup while it is simmering and let the oils from the mint infuse into the simple syrup. When I am done, I merely remove the mint. The variations for infusing your simple syrup are endless. You can use fruit, herbs, spices, chocolate, and so on.

PART 3: PAIRINGS AND COCKTAILS

PAIRINGS

Another way to change a tea is not just to alter what is in the cup with the tea but to change what you eat while drinking the tea. Wine drinkers have known for hundreds of years that a fine wine is best experienced with the perfect food pairing. A nice white Burgundy tastes delicious, but when paired with a duck liver pâté the experience can be transcendent.

Various foods have the same effect with tea. Step off a plane in China and you will discover not only people drinking tea, but people drinking tea and eating seeds. Spend time in the Middle East and discover a plethora of cookies and nuts that pair perfectly with the local style of tea. Similarly, it is rare to find a south Asian family who does not have endless savory snacks to enjoy with their tea.

As the Western world increases its interest in traditional tea, there is an increased interest in discovering what common foods best pair with tea. The options are as diverse as the varieties of tea. With that said, some of my favorite pairings are nuts, seeds, fruit, chocolate, and cheese. Each represents a lifetime of experimentation and discovery as you seek to match the perfect nut, seed, fruit, chocolate, or cheese with your favorite tea. But, as the saying goes, the journey is often more fun than the destination.

As a general rule, fats and salts go really well with an astringent tea because the fat and salt help counter the astringency. Therefore, nuts and seeds are an easy but elegant pairing for an astringent green or black tea such as gunpowder green, or Darjeeling and Bai Lin Congfu black teas. Fruits, on the other hand, tend to go better with a milder tea, such as white teas. I particularly enjoy berries and stone fruits with a light floral white tea such as Bai Mu Dan or Shui Mei. Green teas, on the other hand, tend to pair well with cheese. If you are interested in pairing tea and cheese, it is best to experiment with creamy cow milk cheeses such as Brie, Belstone, or Boursault. Although certainly possible, pairing tea with a saltier aged cheese is very difficult and takes the right pairing because often the earthy, salty aromas of the aged cheese really conflict with the flavor and aroma profiles of tea. Chocolates can also be an interesting pair for tea because the fat negates much of a tea's bitterness while the chocolate's sugar brings out the tea's flavors. Dark chocolates often pair well with panfried green teas such as Longjing (Dragonwell), with a lightly oxidized oolong such as Taiwan's Dung Ding oolong, or with an earthy dark tea such as Pu'erh. Milk chocolate, on the other hand, goes well with more full-bodied teas, especially black teas such as Assam or Dian Hong.

COCKTAILS

Mixing traditional tea drinks is similar to mixing cocktails. So, it was only a matter of time before the two worlds converged—bartenders began incorporating tea into their cocktails, and tea drinkers began wondering what infused teas tasted like with a shot of alcohol. This convergence is beautifully demonstrated in the most unsuspecting places: my hometown of Detroit, Michigan. Annually named one of the hottest and best cocktail centers in the United States and named by *Esquire* magazine as the 2014 Bar City of the Year, Detroit's bartenders are second to none in creating and crafting perfectly balanced, creative, and inspired cocktails.

In wanting to demonstrate not only how to combine the techniques of making an infused tea with alcohol but also to demonstrate the techniques used in the world of cocktails, I challenged Detroit's most acclaimed bartenders to create original tea cocktails to share in this book. In so doing, I wanted to demonstrate the power of working collaboratively and to inspire you to create new traditions, tastes, and experiences with tea.

Austin Nichols
WILD TURKEY
Ancient Age
10
CHARTREUSE
Liqueur du 9e Centenaire
PIMM'S
No1 CUP
PICON
Mount Vernon
Pure Rye
Whiskey
114
OLD GRAND DAD
Old Fitzgerald
W.L.Weller
OLD FITZGERALD
J.W. Dant
ELIJAH CRAIG
12
OLD POTRERO
WHISKEY
OLD FORESTER
Jefferson's Reserve
RUSSELL'S RESERVE
SINGLE BARREL
Four Roses
SINGLE BARREL

SERVES ONE

THE OAKLAND'S EASTERN MARKET TODDY

INGREDIENTS

- 1 tablespoon (6 g) Darjeeling black tea
- 2 teaspoons (4 g) dried lemon peel
- 1 teaspoon dried licorice root
- ½ cup (120 ml) water
- ¼ ounce (7 ml) palm sugar syrup
- 2 ounces (60 ml) Bombay gin
- Grains of paradise sugar (enough to coat the rim of the glass)
- Cinnamon stick for garnish

Tea is often mistaken for any warm beverage made with spices. Therefore, it is natural to infuse the traditional hot toddy with tea. Although hot toddies are typically made with whiskey, sugar, lemon, and spices, the Eastern Market Toddy incorporates gin to provide the requisite alcohol and to add its distinctive aromatics.

To make an infused Darjeeling tea, combine the black tea, lemon peel, and licorice root in a small pot. In another small pot, warm water to 200°F (93°C). Pour the warm water into the pot with the tea and spices and steep for 3 minutes. Mix the warm tea with the palm sugar syrup and Bombay gin. Coat the rim of a glass with sugar, pour the tea into the glass, and garnish with a cinnamon stick.

Read any "best of" list regarding bars, cocktails, or bartenders in North America and you are likely to see The Oakland. With two of its bartenders winning multiple national and international cocktail competitions, The Oakland has helped push innovative cocktail culture into never-before-seen territory and has been integral in shining the international spotlight on Detroit's unique take on crafting cocktails. In accepting my challenge to create a tea-based cocktail, head bartender Chas Williams created a beautifully contemporary hot toddy that he named the Eastern Market Toddy. The Eastern Market Toddy demonstrates how traditional tea-making methods can be paired with traditional cocktail-making methods to create a delicious cocktail.

SERVES ONE

INGREDIENTS

- 2 ounces (60 ml) Assam-Infused Aged Rum (see recipe)
- 2 ounces (60 ml) whole milk
- ¾ ounce (21 ml) Masala Syrup (see recipe)
- 1 egg white
- Ice
- Nutmeg (optional)
- Cinnamon (optional)

SELDEN STANDARD'S DEWAN'S DEATHBED PUNCH

Often overlooked outside of its birthplace in New Orleans, a milk punch cocktail is a perfect cocktail style with which to incorporate tea. A traditional New Orleans milk punch uses milk, brandy, sugar, vanilla, and sometime a garnish of nutmeg. It goes without saying that but for the brandy, a traditional milk punch uses the same ingredients as an English- or Dutch-style tea. Using rum for its sweet and sugary characteristic, Dewan's Deathbed Punch showcases how the two traditions mirror one another.

Combine infused rum, milk, syrup, and egg white in a cocktail shaker and aggressively shake the ingredients to emulsify. Unseal the shaker, add a generous scoop of ice, and shake again. Strain the drink into a rocks glass with fresh ice. Garnish with grated nutmeg or cinnamon.

ASSAM-INFUSED AGED RUM

- Assam or Ceylon black tea
- Aged rum such as Thomas Tew, El Dorado 12, or Zaya

In a clean jar, add 1 tablespoon (6 g) of Assam or Ceylon black tea to 6 ounces (175 ml) of aged rum and let sit for 12 to 24 hours. When the rum is fully infused, strain the rum into a clean container and refrigerate until use. If you use a particularly sweet, vanilla-flavored rum, you may wish to use less than the specified amount of masala syrup in the final drink to avoid a cloying drink.

MASALA SYRUP

- 1 cup (235 ml) water
- 1 cup (200 g) sugar
- 1 tablespoon (6 g) crushed black peppercorns
- 1 tablespoon (5 g) coriander seeds
- 10 to 12 cloves
- 10 cardamom pods, cracked
- 1 or 2 cinnamon sticks

In a small pot, combine water, sugar, peppercorns, coriander seeds, cloves, cardamom pods, and cinnamon sticks. Heat the mixture until the sugar is dissolved. Remove from heat and let cool. Keep refrigerated until ready to use.

In 2014, Detroit's farm-to-table restaurant Selden Standard was named one of the most-anticipated restaurants to open in the United States. Created by a chance encounter between Evan Hansen and chef Andy Hollyday, Selden Standard epitomizes the city's reputation as a hotbed for creative dining and extraordinary cocktails. Selden Standard operates on a rotating menu that changes when the season dictates, changes reflected not only with the food created by Chef Hollyday but also through the irreproachable cocktail menu created by Evan Hansen. Using only locally sourced ingredients, Hansen has kept his bar menu in line with the ethos of the restaurant itself: casual fare, meticulously prepared. This ethos can be seen in Evan's tea-based twist on the traditional milk punch he sardonically named Dewan's Deathbed Punch.

THE SUGAR HOUSES'S GIN DEATH'S DOOR

SERVES ONE

INGREDIENTS

- ½ ounce yellow chartreuse
- ½ ounce grapefruit, fresh squeezed
- ½ ounce honey dissolved in warm water (50/50 ratio)
- 6 ounces steamed green tea (preferably sencha)

Made with 130 herbs, plants and flowers, Chartreuse is named after the Grande Chartreuse monastery in Grenoble France.

Although uncommon outside of France, Chartreuse is essentially a fermented apothecary, making it the perfect spirit to use in this drink that combines tea traditions of Korea (fresh fruit), Western Europe / North America (honey), and Japan (sencha green tea). Of course, what is a good cocktail in the early twenty-first century without an ironic name like Gin Death's Door?

To make the Sugar Houses's Gin Death's Door, simply combine all the ingredients and shake over ice.

Opening in 2011 at the apex of the craft cocktail craze in the United States, the Sugar House and its owner, David Kwiatkowski, wanted to bring to Detroit the concepts and techniques highlighted in other craft cocktail lounges in the United States, such as the Violet Hour in Chicago and Milk & Honey in New York. With their attention to detail and commitment to quality, the Sugar House almost instantly began being mentioned in the same breath as the most famous craft cocktail bars. More important, the Sugar House became one of the anchor establishments that brought international acclaim to Detroit's craft cocktail scene. In fact, in 2013, one of the Sugar House's bartenders, Yani Frye, won the Angostura Bitters Cocktail Challenge U.S. Finals, bringing even more notoriety to this highly focused craft cocktail bar. Sugar House is both meticulous and adventurous, making cocktails that are as much a revelation as works of art.

Cliff Bell's opened in 1935 as Detroit's most luxurious club and restaurant and was an icon in the city's center throughout most of the twentieth century. But in 1985, as the city suffered from severe disinvestment, the famous mahogany and brass club closed and became just another lost memory. In 2005, current owners Paul Howard, Scott Lowell, and Carolyn Howard, with the help of their friends, neighbors, and family members, tirelessly worked to resurrect the landmark. In just six short months and endless hours of rehab construction, the team reopened the famous club to international acclaim. Since its reopening, Cliff Bell's has routinely been labeled as a must-see restaurant and as one of the best jazz clubs in the United States. Walk into this sensual mahogany and brass-accented club and find yourself transported to a time when cocktails symbolized the life of the country's elite. Staying true to their traditions, the bartenders at Cliff Bell's created a twist on the classic whiskey sour cocktail that they cleverly named the Steep Cliff!

CLIFF BELL'S STEEP CLIFF

Traditionally made with three parts whiskey, two parts bitter, and one part sugar, the whiskey sour is one of the most, if not the most, famous of North American cocktails. With the Western world's penchant for strong, bitter black tea mixed with sugar, the Steep Cliff represents a contemporary twist on the old classic.

SERVES ONE

INGREDIENTS

- 2 ounces (60 ml) bourbon
- 1½ ounces (42 ml) strong black tea such as Assam or Ceylon
- ¾ ounce (20 ml) simple syrup
- ¾ ounce (20 ml) fresh lime juice
- Ice
- Maraschino cherry

Add the bourbon, tea, syrup, and lime juice to a collins glass filled with ice. Sake vigorously and garnish with a Maraschino cherry.

SERVES ONE

WOODBRIDGE PUB'S WORLD WAR TEA

When the world thinks of Americans, they often think of excess and irreverence. The World War Tea combines both of these attributes into a tea-infused irreverent twist on the very American cocktail known as the Long Island Iced Tea.

INGREDIENTS

- 1½ ounces (42 ml) Ciroc peach vodka
- 1½ ounces (42 ml) limoncello
- 1 ounce (28 ml) Barenjager
- Ice
- Lemonade
- Black tea
- Lemon wedge for garnish

Pour the Ciroc peach, limoncello, and Barenjager over ice in a pint glass and add equal parts lemonade and black tea. Garnish with a lemon wedge.

If you seek a restaurant where the locals of all ages gather, look no further than Detroit's Woodbridge Pub. Dedicated to supporting local businesses and artists, the Woodbridge Pub has a reputation for its warm spirit, creative menu, and clever take on traditional cocktails. It is no wonder that when challenged to create a tea-based cocktail, the bartenders at the Woodbridge Pub created this tongue-in-cheek-named cocktail World War Tea, a cocktail you could find in any local pub or restaurant in North America.

ACKNOWLEDGMENTS

A heartfelt thanks goes to my daughters, Jaya Samina and Meera Jyothi, who continually remind me that life's pleasures come in the simplest packages; my wife, Sunita Doddamani, for agreeing to walk by my side on our incredible journey; my parents, Joe and Mary Uhl, for providing me the freedom to become comfortable seeking the unknown; and my in-laws Gadigeppa and Prabha Doddamani for their continued help and sacrifice.

Thank you to Marvin Shaouni for following me to the other side of the world to photograph some of the world's most beautiful regions and for sharing those photographs in this book.

Thank you to everyone who allowed me to tell their story and share their recipes in this book. The dedication they display toward their crafts and skills continually motivates me to give back to our shared communities.

Thank you to Chad Allen, Vijay Hotanahalli, Scott Hill, Paul Wilkes, Cassidy Zobl, Jessica Decker, Jon Dones, Andy Kopietz, Genna Cowsert and Jerald McBride for providing their unique creativity in the Joseph Wesley Black Tea project as well as to the people who agreed to help with the Joseph Wesley Black Tea project even when it was just a vague idea: Clare Pfeiffer, Adam Duke, Tami Slaats, Kathy Lopez, Emma Chen, and Brian Harger.

To my friends who worked without reward, provided invaluable advice, goodwill, companionship, or support while I figured out how to share the art and craft of tea with the world, especially Shawn Santo, Kevin Borsay, Doug Fry, Carter Malcolm, Ian McCulloch, Bryan Curry, Dan Cole, Brian Souders, Almir Horozic, Jen Fitzpatrick, Leslie Calhoun, Hyur Tursun, Micah Loucks, and Johanna Kononen.

Thank you to the team at Quarto Publishing Group USA for helping create this book, especially Jonathan Simcosky for his tolerance of my midwestern sensibilities, Regina Grenier for her dedication to creating a look and feel for the book that respects the art and craft of tea, and Alissa Cyphers for her hours of diligence and effort to fix and edit my writing.

Finally, I would like to thank everyone who graciously shared a cup of tea and a moment of their lives with me.

ABOUT THE PHOTOGRAPHER

Marvin Shaouni is a Detroit-based freelance editorial and commercial photographer specializing in food, portraits, and everyday life.

Shaouni's interest in photographing people and food culture can be traced back to his formative years. First-born, first-generation American, to first-born immigrant parents, his favorite moments were family gatherings, where multiple languages collided joyously (and loudly), combining Spanish, Aramaic, and broken English—not to mention the fragrant aromas of Caribbean and Middle Eastern cuisine pouring out of the kitchen.

When Shaouni is not working or traveling, you can find him trying to teach himself how to play the banjo, clawhammer style. He lives in the predominantly Latino community in southwest Detroit.

Shaouni's work has been featured in *Surface, Food Network Magazine, Imbibe, Conde Nast Traveler, Oprah Magazine, Entrepreneur, Hour Detroit*, and *Inc.* Some of his clients include Shinola, EMI Blue Note Records, Quicken Loans, Issue Media Group, University of Michigan, and Quarto Publishing Group. He is also managing photographer for Model D, a weekly online magazine in Detroit. You can find him at www.marvinshaouni.com.

ABOUT THE AUTHOR

Joe Uhl's passion for tea began in 1992 with an undergraduate study abroad program in Malaysia. He parlayed his time in Malaysia into a lifelong journey. Through subsequent travels and stays in varying corners of the world—Europe, Russia, China, central Asia, Southeast Asia, south Asia, and east Africa—he met remarkable people, many of whom spurred his desire to gain a deeper understanding of tea and tea culture.

Eventually these travels compelled him to find and meet the world's great tea growers, producers, and connoisseurs. These meetings enraptured him in the complex historical, cultural, and philosophical importance of tea.

Uhl learned the art and craft of the world's great tea in some of the most notorious classrooms, including the ancient tea fields of southeast China, the tropical Cameron Highlands of Malaysia, the Nilgiri mountain region of southern India, as well as the colonial tea fields surrounding Kenya's Great Rift Valley. Uhl has meticulously developed a portfolio of tea-related adventures unsurpassed by all but a very few.

This more than twenty-year journey not only brought Uhl to some of the most esteemed growing regions, but it also introduced him to some of the most revered cultures and histories of tea. From sampling yak butter tea with the Mongols in the Pamir Mountains of western China, partaking in England's high tea in London, and cheering the tarik competitors in Southeast Asia, to participating in the age-old debate as to what Indian cities promote the best chai wallahs, Uhl's journey provided him access to some of the most fascinating and endearing stories about tea.

In 2013, Uhl quit his job as an attorney at a large multinational law firm in Detroit and started his tea company, Joseph Wesley Black Tea. Through this company, Uhl has begun sharing the stories that captured his heart as well as sharing some of his favorite teas from some of the most esteemed growing areas and tea producers in the world.

INDEX